The
Curmudgeon
Chronicles

Also by Bert Raynes

*Birds of Grand Teton National Park
and the Surrounding Area*

Finding the Birds of Jackson Hole

Valley So Sweet

Published by:
White Willow Publishing
1255 N. Iron Rock Road #6 • Jackson, Wyoming 83001 • 307-734-7002

ISBN 0-9642423-4-6

The
Curmudgeon
Chronicles

by
Bert Raynes

Foreword
by Michael Sellett
Illustrated by
Rebecca Woods

White Willow Publishing

Foreword

Bert Raynes is an enlightened Luddite.

How else would you describe a man who deftly winds his way through dense intellectual conundrums yet never learned to type? I'm not talking about someone who is computer illiterate; that would be forgivable. I mean someone who never learned to hunt-and-peck on a Smith-Corona.

I first became aware Bert was technologically challenged nearly two decades ago, when he offered to write a column on birds for the *Jackson Hole News*. Our outdoor columnist, Dan Abrams, had founded the Jackson Hole Bird Club and began reporting area bird sightings as an addendum to his popular column. When Abrams retired, Bert jumped into the breach, proposing to keep track of our feathered friends not in a postscript, but as an *entire column.*

Before I land on the Audubon Society's hit list, I want to set the record straight: I don't have anything against birds. At the same time, I had trouble visualizing how anyone could attract a broad readership by reporting the sightings of nuthatches and grosbeaks at backyard feeders around the valley.

I resisted. Bert persisted.

As I have learned over the years, Bert is easy to underestimate. His persistence overcame my resistance and on June 11, 1980, his "Birds in Jackson Hole" made its first appearance in the *News*. In that column—which arrived handwritten on three pages torn from a yellow legal pad—Bert mused how the wet, nasty weather that was making our lives miserable was also taking its toll on the valley's birds.

The interconnectedness of our lives is a theme that has echoed through Bert's column for nearly 20 years. Long before the concept of ecosystem management became fashionable, he explored the relationship between man, the land, and its native creatures.

It is not surprising his writings soon wandered beyond birds. We changed the name of the column to "Field Notes" in the mid-80s to reflect his expanded perspective.

This was the beginning of the end. Nuthatch and grosbeak sightings were gradually relegated to the end of the column, upstaged by wry observations on politics, science, popular culture, and man's foibles. Not content with the limitations implied by "Field Notes," Bert's writings began appearing under the moniker "Far Afield" in 1992.

No matter what logo he was flying under, Bert's illegible scribblings on yellow legal paper faithfully arrived every week—to the dismay of every typesetter who ever worked at the *News*.

And my worries about whether his writings would find an audience proved to be as prescient as the wag who predicted the automobile would never replace the horse and buggy.

Michael Sellett
Publisher, *Jackson Hole News*

Author's Preface

For something like 20 years I have written "Far Afield," a column about natural history and allied topics for the weekly *Jackson Hole News* in Jackson Hole, Wyoming. For some years a number of well-meaning readers have suggested that a compilation of these protean essays would be appreciated and well received.

Since the origins of many of the pieces herein appeared in my column, it has not been overlooked by me that I would be remiss should I fail to express my idea of what a columnist is.

Simple. My idea of a columnist is Russell Baker of the *New York Times*, who once opined:

"It takes great confidence to write a newspaper column. Some might say it takes arrogance. Be that as it may, my willingness to pronounce on a great many matters of which I have little or no knowledge is one of my prime qualifications for this trade."

Amen.

Russell Baker (May I say, Russ?) also confesses to an occasional mistake. I don't often own up. Yet, terminological inexactitudes happen. Column writing is, afterall, a kind of journalism: the last refuge of the vaguely talented. I herewith accept responsibility for at least a couple of mistakes in two decades. One I remember had to do with something concerning space and astronomical distances. Had I been correct, Earth would have been destroyed. I forget the other. Probably something equally trivial. So, I've owned up. If you find a mistake in this book, tell the publisher. Only fair.

While Russ never reprinted them, I obey these rules of writing (and I think RB does, too):

- Avoid cliches like the plague.
- Try to not split infinitives.
- A pronoun must reflect their antecedents.

Were my column syndicated, I might try to dazzle readers in the manner of William Buckley, Jr. or Georgie Will, producing feuilletons spiced with a soupcon of espieglerie. I'd avoid oscitancy, fribbling topics, tautologic sentiments and dithyrambs.

But, heck. I don't write to impress or bewilder folks. My columns appear in a small weekly newspaper in a town of northwest Wyoming. They are designed to lead readers to the path or wisdom and enlightenment.

It's my code of ethics.

•

Many of the causeries that follow weren't intended to be published in an anthology. Credit, if such it is, goes to The Muse of the column, my wife Meg. Although her urgings to do another book—regardless of subject—may have been simply to get me to do *something* around the house, she always lends her special talents to making my thoughts intelligible and scribbles legible.

I'm grateful as well to Mike Sellett, publisher and owner of the *Jackson Hole News*, and his entire staff. Winning Mike over to the idea of a viable bird— and later, all-encompassing natural history column—was like straightening the Tower of Pisa: It had to be done slowly and with exquisite subtlety. He has been generous in permitting me to write about anything I believe will appeal to my readers. If not generous in honoraria. Further, he accepts handwritten copy, which must then be "put into" whatever those insipid-looking, putty-faced machines with a single cathode-ray eye feed on, later to go into whatever has replaced the linotype machines of my youth. I take that acceptance, albeit grudging, as a sign of editorial approval. If it isn't, I don't want to hear about it.

I have special gratitude for my faithful readers. Thanks, too, to a multitude of generous folks who urged me to do another book, especially including the fellows in The Deaf-As-A-Post Lunch Bunch, Jan Hayse and Jan Herbst. Their continued interest and that of other good friends was a source of inspiration, as was the encouragement of my publisher, Becky Woods. Becky actually both smothered me (initially) with TLC but also prodded in the manner of a sand grain with an oyster.

I acknowledge that I can be cranky, grouchy, and curmudgeonly and—as a result of writing weekly columns—that this can occur rather chronically. So to speak. I don't know if this is how Becky came up with the title, but she was bound and determined to keep it.

Thus and herewith, *The Curmudgeon Chronicles*. As Dorothy Parker remarked, "This is not a novel to be tossed aside lightly. It should be thrown with great force."

Toss it. Throw it. Love it. Leave it. But first, read it.

Let me know if you like it. Otherwise, fuggedaboutit.

Bert Raynes
Jackson Hole, Wyoming
1998

Contents

Curmudgeon

Defining terms

The entry for January 1 in the 1993 Daily Curmudgeon Calendar is, "Day, n. A period of twenty-four hours, mostly misspent. — Ambrose Pierce."

I know this because I received the Curmudgeon Calendar as a Christmas gift from the Jackson Hole Post Office staff. Presented personally by Postmaster Al Berglund with appropriate remarks.

Now, I keep my post office drawer orderly and neat; I wipe my boots when entering the facility. I almost always display the appropriate mixture of hope, resignation, patience, trepidation and wonderment when dallying in line at the desk. I rigorously limit my complaints-to-Al to no more than one a month.

I shall continue to do so. For I deeply appreciate this gift, this gesture. Curmudgeon is defined right up front in this calendar as "1. *archaic:* a crusty, ill-tempered, churlish old man, or 2. *modern:* anyone who hates hypocrisy and pretense and has the temerity to say so; anyone with the habit of pointing out unpleasant facts in an engaging and humorous manner."

Well, sure. Them's me, baby.

Incidentally, the cantankerous quote for April 21, 1993, is by Woody Allen: "Love is the answer, but while you're waiting for the answer, sex raises some pretty good questions."

Now, um, under which segment of that little old definition does he fit again?

Archaic

While trying, futilely, to tidy up at least a few odds and ends, I could not help noticing that the word "grumbled" and my name appeared in the same sentence in an article in one of our local newspapers. Well, hell's bells.

I have heard rumors and suggestions to the effect that I can be curmudgeonly on, ah, rare occasions, so I have considered this to be, certainly, a possibility. After all, I'm only human. But in print!

Thus, I inquired of my lovely wife, a.k.a. The Muse, if she could think of, say, as many as three matters, subjects, situations or circumstances that might cause me to express a displeasure.

She took the Fifth Amendment. She isn't renowned as a Muse without good reason.

After much reflection, introspection and meditation—not to mention medication—I came up with a very few. They all seem mostly to relate to my early education, during which I was taught to respect my elders, appreciate the English language, leave at least a little space between my front bumper and the rear bumper ahead, respect other people's property and the desire for privacy, and follow baseball.

It's far too late, I suspect, for me to alter what is ingrained concerning these general topics. I could, I suppose, with great determination, try to camouflage my feelings better than apparently I do...

Next year. For sure.

•

Grumpy Old Men

A hot news item announced a film featuring actors Jack Lemmon and Walter Matthau. They are growing old, sometimes together, and will star is a new picture entitled *Grumpy Old Men*. Intrigued, I remarked that perhaps I should apply. The Muse recommended — rather flatly I thought — that I should see if they needed a role model.

Whichever.

On the Road Again

✎

Southern California

We made a trip to Los Angeles once, to visit the La Brea Tar Pits. A kind of pilgrimage, I guess, for we had read a lot about them and the trapped creatures whose bones are preserved there. We'd been there, done that; so much, I thought, for that town.

Perhaps not. I've recently learned that the Museum of Jurassic Technology opened in L.A. a half dozen years ago. Whatever else it has on display, there's one exhibit which should be — to say the very least — intriguing to read about. Quoting from "The Sophisticated Travelers," a *New York Times* magazine supplement,

"An exhibit called 'Bernard Maston, Donald R. Griffith and the Drepong Mori of the Tripiscum Plateau' portrays the discovery of a tiny bat that emits X-rays and is therefore able to fly through solid objects."

I'm reasonably sure I have never seen one of those animals.

The museum has other marvels, too, including the explanation of the "theory of obliscence" of one Geoffrey Sonnabend, who states there is no such thing as memory. He proves it with a model demonstrating "the cone of confabulation, the perverse and obverse atomic discs, spelean ring disparity and the attitude and altitude of experience." All this and more at the Museum of Jurassic Technology, 9341 Venice Boulevard in L.A. Open Thursdays through Sundays.

If you get there, would you pick up a brochure and maybe a souvenir from the gift shop for us? Oh, we're tempted to go, but our passports to Southern California may no longer be valid.

•

Yemen

I see by an AP report that "Yemen is the World's best place to be kidnapped." It seems that nearly 100 foreigners have been kidnapped there in the past four years by armed tribesmen.

The tribesmen are angry at government neglect; in exchange for their hostages, they are given government projects or jobs. The hostages often emerge "in high spirits, sometimes with gifts of curved daggers or Arab robes from their gracious captors."

Well, gee. I'm thinking of taking a dozen or so adventurous bird watchers on a Yemen tour. Y'know, when the hawks and whatever the heck else birds there may be in Yemen, are in Yemen (wherever the heck Yemen is). We'll supply all the fresh pita bread and rice and goat you can eat. Not to mention a chance to receive a jambiya: You can't get traditional daggers just anywhere, anymore.

It will probably take some time to arrange all this—some disconsolate tribesmen don't promptly answer their faxes—but get your reservation* in now.

*Note: Hostage training emphasizing fear response and groveling will be required.

Somewhere in Idaho

Travel should be a learning experience. Travel by automobile — if it takes one off the interstate to out-of-the-way small towns — can open your eyes. In a small Idaho town (which I shall not name because who knows?, we may wish to return) we read the twice-a-week little paper over break fast. Circulation a surprising 6,400.

Skipping over the politics and scandals, below are selected items from the April 21, 1992, issue:

"There are some birthdays today. Fascinating, isn't it? Who is celebrating here in the valley? Why, it's Betty H_____, of course. Happy birthday, Betty. May you get lots of good stuff."

And, "Did anything take place on this date? Why sure. And it was a long time ago, too, that Chicago outlawed hogs in the city limits — 1843 in fact. Then in 1857 Al Douglas patented the bustle, followed by the Spanish American War."

Personally, I like the guy's style. It has punch, class, individuality, a penchant for putting two-and-two together to make something. He had paragraphs under sub-headings that included Sexual Abuse, Good Nutrition, Getting Organized, and The New York Mets Baseball Team.

I got excited when I saw a classified ad headlined "Body Parts." Turned out to be parts for a '68 Ford half ton.

Breakfast was a disappointment, too.

•

Where Are We? Or, "Let's Ask that Guy."

Nature study sometimes requires — even encourages — traveling obscure back roads. Back a ways we did just that. Many of the maps we consulted showed faint dots and dashes over large areas, below which was printed cryptic advice: Make Local Inquiry.

It didn't take long to learn not to expect inhabitants in most of these areas. Or find anybody in nearby Off Center to be awake before 10 a.m. Or to expect very much. Pretty much in that order. If we passed the first two hurdles, we got an, ah, enlightening response. To wit:

▸ What road? One over No-Return Pass? It's okay. Went over it in '64, right after I got back from 'Nam. Didn't have no problem.

▸ Where?? Oh. Yeah. Guess it's okay. Saw a pickem'up go that way last week, guess it was, and never seen it come back. Guess they got through.

Hey, Pa! Some people here want to see some damn duck. What'll I tell them?

- Your outfit? To Elephant Breath? You'll make it. Heard they're done blasting that mountain to its knees.
- Lived here 53 years. Never been that way. Don't like it over there.
- Only been here three days. I dunno. (This help usually comes from civil servants, as the designation is.)
- Rain? Gee, haven't heard. Only radio we get here comes from Radio Free Bulgaria and plays jungle music real loud. RFB says it'll be real nice for the next coupla...Those clouds? Nothing to 'em. We get clouds like that ever'day this timeayear. Don't mean nothin.
- Wal, ya go down past Zeke's place. On your left. Take a little jog to your right — No, your left — and ease down to the crick. It should be low this month. Pull up to where the old cafe wuz and you'll see this little track going kinda north by northwest into the tules and ya take that. Opens up after a coupla miles. Oughta see some bighorns on the rocks there.
- Yeah, I SEE your damn map, but there ain't no road there. If I were you I'd go back down here, see, to Missing Gap...
- I never have no problem with my outfit. What? Oh, old surplus 6-by. Flotation tires. Exhaust stacks.
- Ain't no birds or animals there after 5 p.m. when I close the gates.
- Dammit, how-in-hell should I know? I'm here marking up the prices you idiots from the big cities'll pay for everything and anything and I don't have no time for silly questions. Buy something or get out.
- No problem 'cept for the dust if its dry. You won't move at all if it's wet. Rain?? Seems to me it rained — hell, was that yesterday or over the weekend? Say, Martha...
- I wouldn't go there. Nothin there. Ain't nuthin' we don't got here.
- It don't go nowhere. Just to that lookout place. All you do is look over

some mountains. I never saw nobody there. Sometimes a big cat. Think they call it a coo-ger or something.

▸ Go there?? Hell mister, there ain't no thru to go thru to. Must be 40 miles. Ain't a soul over there. Just go back down to here and pick up I-4000 NW, and...

▸ What year map you got? That's a 4-lane blacktop now. They leveled Mt. Idy and pushed it into Pleasant Lake and built condos and shopping malls onto 'em. Why they got this shopping mall which has a real live brontosaurus in it you can ride and...

▸ Why youse askin' me? Do I look like a travel guide?

▸ Here you go, free distribution state map. Only a buck-and-a-half.

▸ You one-a-them bird watchers? Ha, ha. Say, where's your funny hat and rubber boots and...

▸ Hey listen, you can't get there from here.

▸ Can't miss it. No problem.

•

Say Please

Once upon a time we had a classic Jeep station wagon, one of those high boxy affairs of the post-war, pre-Humvee period. We had retrofitted it, enjoying, in hindsight, a time in the history of automotive design when a person could drill holes in a car body, attach various things to bumpers and actually personalize a car. Today a guy can't find a place to hide a spare key so it will be lost forever, and "personalized" means an optional paint job.

The Jeep had a water pump mounted on a fender, spare gas can holders behind the fenders, and an interior arrangement by which we could extend a plywood bed capable of accommodating two people of our size. And shape. The latter improvement required a structure built over our permanently extended rear window and tailgate. It was a doozy.

In it we took backroads and no roads, and only came to any sizable town for provisions. When we did, we'd see other rigs with special additions that we openly admired, while graciously answering queries about ours. It was fun, but primarily we wanted to be out on our own, without company of any kind. We and our puppy.

On one such off-road trip in the southwest, we were jouncing along a rutted track near Monument Valley, Utah, enjoying the desert sky, the vistas, the rock formations. We were almost alone; now and then, a flock of sheep herded by a woman on horseback would come and go in a bleating cloud of dust.

As we rounded Thunderbird Mesa we were suddenly, unexpectedly, at the periphery of an amazing array of vehicles, humans and assorted paraphernalia. Trucks, trailers, cars, tables, cameras, people on top of people. Semi-trailers that housed toilets and staircases. Black extension cords spaghettied on the desert floor.

And standing ahead of us, an apparition out of a 1950s Hollywood production set. (And why not? It *was* the 50s.) Slight build, turtleneck sweater, beret, sharply creased pants. Holding up an imperious manicured hand, he glared pompously at us before announcing, "You will have to stop here or turn around. We are shooting a commercial and you are in the scene!"

No "please." Just that pre-emptory demand.

Looking around, we saw that we indeed were in the proposed scene. Just off to one side, previously unnoticed by us in the hub-bub, was a brand-new Ford Thunderbird convertible. A guy sporting a wool dress jacket and a whole faceful of sparkling white, capped teeth was behind the wheel. He was obviously ready to do whatever he was supposed to do.

I leaned out of our window, looked the thing addressing us over carefully, and allowed that unless, and until, he or somebody higher up asked us PLEASE to move on, our plan was to park right there and change a tire. And that changing a tire on this jeep meant taking out almost all our gear to get to the jack and the spare. Might take 3-4 hours, what with lunch and all.

It was kind of funny to watch the parade of emotion that flitted across the flagman/production assistant/brother-in-law's face. Anger, rage, resistance—and after a consultation with himself and cameramen, guys with flags and just more guys—resignation.

He said *please* . The actor-driver said, *"please, please."* (He was hot in his wool jacket.)

And so we moved as grandly as we could with an oddly-configured, dust covered Jeep, through the movie set and past a fringe of spectators both annoyed and mildly amused. We weren't offered lunch or a potty break.

But then we didn't ask.

The episode sensitized us thereafter to the implausible arrogance of movie and commercial film crews. They invariably consider their interests to be unquestionably more important than anyone else's. Somehow, so do most people, even when inconvenienced. Speed demons who will tailgate anyone not going 10 miles over the speed limit will park it without a question for a film outfit. Folks who get apoplectic at road construction delays are accommodating when confronted by Hollywood people.

Not us. Not any longer. I am sanguine about tourist jams and people stopping haphazardly to view wildlife or a scenic spot. While I don't intellectually accept the clearly over-manned work crews used in road construction, I understand the delays required and calmly idle away the lost hours. A lost traveler has my sympathy, not antagonism. And a person attempting to find a parking spot needs luck, not a horn.

But I don't cut any slack to rude film-makers.

Truth to tell, the issue doesn't rear its ugly head very often. The last time was several years ago, when Ford Motors, again, was making a commercial in our little subdivision. Some guy attempted to keep us from going to our home.

Yeah. Right.

•

Give Me A Sign

Pop quiz: Which occupation creates such self-absorption that its practitioners are oblivious to all stimuli other than those directly affecting their own interests (excluding skiers, of course)? My answer, for personal reasons, is highway engineers. Civil engineers and real estate developers are tied for a close second.

Ignore actual highway design with inadequate base and lousy drainage. Forget surfaces that deteriorate in one winter season, two at most. Set aside hazardous roads and intersections that remain such until a set number of people die. Forget those things. Think, instead, of highway signs.

Signage is the correct term, but correctness isn't a pertinent concern to signage folks, one concludes. How else to explain signs which tell you St. Louis is 400 miles, then 250 miles, then 130, then 90, 70, 60, 43, 27, 18, and *just then*, drop St. Louis and switch to names only a local could possibly recognize. Elephant's Breath 1 mile; Squeaky Springs, 1.5651 miles ahead.

What happened to old St. Louey? It has been replaced by Nashville, which, of course, is nowhere near the neighborhood.

I've yet to conquer Next Exit signage. "Gas and grease, Next Exit" appears, and I sail right by This Exit, which I realize what was actually meant once I'm already past it. No Kentucky Fried for this boy. I've taken to packing a food hamper.

No signage is as irritating as poor signage. Grandma moved and you're trying to follow an unfamiliar rural road to get there as promised. You come to a tee intersection with no signs. None. So you decide to go right, and after seven or eight miles reach barricades announcing "Road Closed." There is, of course, no place easily to turn around, say, your U-Haul truck.

Scenic Highway designation draws flocks of people intent on driving 75 mph, scenery aside, and I'm convinced that "Scenic View" signs are former construction turn-outs where the road crews parked their equipment and vehicles. We leave the camera in the car at Scenic Views. We've learned.

"Wildlife Viewing Area" tickles me. I wonder if anyone bothered to tell the critters. Apparently not. My guess is that once, perhaps in 1960 or '62, a fox trotted across the very meadow before you. Of course, that was before the Fox and Vixen Shopping Mall was built across the way.

Then there are the ubiquitous little blue signs that tell you where to set your AM and FM radio dials to get weather information. Did you ever try that? Either you get static, or a radio station that plays what Ed Abbey called "music to pound out fenders by," otherwise known as rock 'n roll.

But I digress. In fact, I've lost my way. A good sign would be helpful. You can bet I'm not holding my breath.

The King's Language

Ya know what I mean?

Charles, Prince of Wales, no doubt has figured out that he is going to be quite an old gent before he gets to be King of England, so he's set about finding other things to do. He's been advocating conservation of the earth's wildlife and environments — of all fool things — and taking on British architects, pointing out designs that are ugly, or overwhelming, or out-of-place.

Now he's upset with a "modern version" rewrite of the 1552 *Book of Common Prayer*. Asked Charlie, rhetorically, "Is it entirely an accident that the defacing of Cranmer's prayer book has coincided with a calamitous decline in literacy and the quality of English?"

Here's the Prince's illustration of Hamlet's soliloquy, the one which begins "To be or not to be..." , if done in this new style:

"Well, frankly, the problem as I see it
At this moment in time, is whether I
Should just lie down under all this hassle
And let them walk all over me,
Or, whether I should just say:
Okay, I get the message,
And do myself in.
I mean, let's face it,
I'm in a no-win situation,
And quite honestly,

I'm so stuffed up to here
With the whole stupid mess,
I can tell you,
I've just got a good mind to take
The quick way out.
That's the bottom line.
The only problem is: What happens
If I find that
When I've bumped myself off,
There's some kind of a
You know
All that mystical stuff
About when you die
You might find you're still —
You know what I mean?"

•

Nine Little Words

My attention was directed recently to an article by Cullen Murphy in the March, 1988, *Atlantic* magazine. It concerned a lexicographer named G.H. McKnight who, in 1923, determined to identify the English words most commonly used in conversation, and how often the most commonly used words appear. Mr. McKnight concluded that out of some 600,000 to 800,000 words, a mere 43 account for fully half the words spoken.

Moreover, a mere nine words account for fully one-quarter of all English spoken *and* written. The Big Nine: *and, be, have, it, of, the, to, will* and *you*. Reviewing this finding, Mr. Murphy was incredulous, concluding, "This is the kind of preposterous scientific claim that fairly cries out for indepen-dent scrutiny."

He proceeded to examine a number of what can be fairly described as eclectic English-language texts, including: *The Mayflower Compact,* "Jabberwocky," Spiro Agnew's letter of resignation, "The Marine's Hymn," the first five verses of Saint Paul's *Epistle to the Galatians,* the Miranda Rights which were — in 1988, anyhow — required to be read to a suspect, a section chosen at random from the owner's manual for a 1987 Colt Vista ("Flooded Engine"), and the introduction to "Internal Revenue Publication 920."

You guessed it: McKnight was right on. In the texts examined, the Big Nine accounted for 21.4-35.4 percent of all words; the average was 27.4 percent.

Murphy noted that the word "please" and expression "thank you" don't make it into conversation very often these days.

Murphy is obviously a very wry fellow. I would like to find out what he thinks the phrase "excuse me" means to so many who mutter it. To me it seems to mean, "Look out, Mac, I'm coming through."

•

The Power of Words

When Toni Morrison received the 1993 Nobel Prize in Literature early in December, she addressed the academy. I wish I could have been there.

Morrison spoke eloquently of the value of language as words. Words, she said, empower meditation; words fend off the "scariness of things that have no names;" and it is words that enable us to make sense of our exist-ence by allowing us to stand aside to narrate it.

"We die," she observed. "That may be the meaning of life. But we do language. That may be the measure of our lives."

Morrison reminded her audience that language can die. It can be killed. It can be drafted into the army of oppressors and become an instrument of domination. "Oppressive language does more than represent violence," she noted, "it is violence; does more than represent the limits of knowledge: It limits knowledge."

Morrison declared that if used correctly, language can illuminate, can delineate, can "limn the actual, imagined and possible lives of its speakers, readers, writers."

Remember that when some self-styled educator-type tries to convince you that it really doesn't matter whether kids — or teachers — use correct grammar, or can write a sentence, or can read proficiently, or can spell.

•

Oops.

Actual headlines. Collected by actual journalists.
▸ Something Went Wrong in Jet Crash, Safety Expert Says
▸ Safety Experts Say School Bus Passengers Should Be Belted
▸ Stud Tries Out, Panda Mating Fails: Veterinarian Takes Over
▸ New Study of Obesity Looks for Larger Test Group
▸ Astronaut Takes Blame for Gas in Spacecraft
▸ Local High School Dropouts Cut in Half

•

Lie. Lay. Cool.

On a single day in July, 1995, I read that the gene that caused bed wetting had been isolated, and listened as a Baby Boomer TV reporter gave up on the formerly understood, but more and more mysterious, difference between lie and lay. She announced that someone did "lie the gun on the table."

I thought on that otherwise pleasant day that—whereas I previously had looked forward to learning at least one new thing each day—perhaps these two items alone could satisfy my entire July quota. There are, after all, things one learns that he could just as well have foregone.

Now then: Bed wetting is a problem about 10 percent of children suffer and was, until this discovery, considered to be primarily emotional. I suspect this finding won't soon dispel this conception. Too bad.

As to whether a distinction exists or needs to be made between lie and lay, it appears no one cares any longer. The Muse advised me long ago that nobody admires a pedant and simply to forget it and lie or lay back and relax.

Whatever.

Cool.

•

For Sale
▸ Four-poster bed, 101 years old. Perfect for antique lover.
▸ Have several very old dresses from grandmother in beautiful condition.
▸ Tired of cleaning yourself? Let me do it.
▸ Auto Repair Service. Free pick up and delivery. Try us once. You'll never go anywhere again.
▸ Dog for sale. Eats anything and is fond of children

Say What?

The Oakland School Board recently suggested that, in fairness, black school children should be taught in ebonic—a rough, street language—in school, and that this language be officially recognized.

Reaction was swift and divided. Internet wags, however, pointed out that a whole host of new "languages" are already being taught in Oakland. To wit:

> Irish-American Speak: Leprechaunics
> Native-American Speak: Kimosabics
> Italo-American Speak: Rigatonics
> Chinese-American Speak: Won-tonics
> Japanese-American Speak: Mama-san-tics
> Polish-American Speak: Kielbasanics
> Jewish-American Speak: Zionics
> German-American Speak: Teutonics
> French-American Speak: Escargonics
> Oakland School Board Speak: Moronics

•

Cursing Made Easy

Perhaps you have acquired this small volume of cranky essays in a used book store and wondered when it was perpetrated. Saving you time needed to flip through introductory pages for publication date, it was about a year before 2000.

Instead of trying to look ahead and make predictions—which will sound silly a few years down the line—I've been thinking of how we in America are ending the 20th century. In particular, about how our airwaves, cables, satellite transmissions, books, magazines, newspaper and cyberspace are rife with words and expressions that, as a child, I couldn't find in ordinary dictionaries. I had to sneak into my doctor's office and peek in his medical texts. It wasn't very satisfactory, actually, but what was a pre-teen to do? We weren't allowed in "that" section of the reference room of public libraries. The result was that I knew some pretty spiffy words for my age — and didn't comprehend most of them.

Now many of these words and phrases are in everyday usage, murmured by innocent-appearing lips. Shouted across playgrounds. Plastered in newspaper and magazine headlines. Pronounced by TV pundits. Bandied at bridge clubs and church socials. Laughed over in barbershops and booze parlors.Quite an achievement for the 20th century, hey?

I am aware that this is an opportunity for me to finally use these once-forbidden words in my prose. Just for information, naturally — not for prurient purposes.

I pass. You can satisfy your curiosity visiting any middle school, standing in a supermarket checkout line, listening to 24-hour cable news programming or, I'm told, viewing certain Internet sites.

I'm not a prude. I swear on occasions when it is clearly indicated, and sometimes when it isn't. I have picked up *Playboy* with no intent of reading the articles.

But I've also walked out on movies whose dialog is 80-plus percent composed of variations of one particular, four-letter, familiar vulgarity. I almost bless my diminished hearing when certain conversations take place in my presence.

At century's end I am weary of Washington, D.C. scandal. Like vulgar language, scandals have become established in our society. By the time you come upon this book, they may have made political service an unacceptable career for our best and brightest. I hope I'm full of crap in this prospectus.

Continuing Education

You're In

    The essay below was written by an applicant wishing to attend New York University. I'm not sure when he was applying, but if he's out of college now, and available, and I were in a position to offer him a job, it would be his.

    3A Essay: In order for the admissions staff of our college to get to know you, the applicant, better, we ask that you answer the following question: Are there any significant experiences you have had, or accomplishments you have realized, that have helped to define you as a person?

    "I am a dynamic figure, often seen scaling walls and crushing ice. I have been known to remodel train stations on my lunch breaks, making them more efficient in the area of heat retention. I translate ethnic slurs for Cuban refugees, I write award-winning operas. I manage time efficiently. Occasionally, I tread water for three days in a row.

    "I woo women with my sensuous and godlike trombone playing, I can pilot bicycles up severe inclines with unflagging speed, and I cook Thirty-Minute brownies in 20 minutes. I am an expert in stucco, a veteran in love, and an outlaw in Peru.

    "Using only a hoe and a large glass of water, I once single-handedly defended a small village in the Amazon Basin from a horde of ferocious army ants. I play bluegrass cello. I was scouted by the Mets. I am the subject of numerous documentaries. When I'm bored, I build large suspension bridges in my yard. I enjoy urban hang gliding. On Wednesdays, after school, I repair electrical appliances free of charge.

"I am an abstract artist, a concrete analyst, and a ruthless bookie. Critics worldwide swoon over my original line of corduroy evening wear. I don't perspire. I am a private citizen, yet I receive fan mail. I have been caller number nine and have won the weekend passes. Last summer I toured New Jersey with a traveling centrifugal-force demonstration. I bat .400. My deft floral arrangements have earned me fame in international botany circles. Children trust me.

"I can hurl tennis rackets at small moving objects with deadly accuracy. I once read *Paradise Lost, Moby Dick* and *David Copperfield* in one day and still had time to refurbish an entire dining room that evening. I know the exact location of every food item in the supermarket. I have performed several covert operations for the CIA. I sleep once a week; when I do sleep, I sleep in a chair. While on vacation in Canada, I successfully negotiated with a group of terrorists who had seized a small bakery. The laws of physics do not apply to me.

"I balance, I weave, I dodge, I frolic, and my bills are paid. On weekends, to let off steam, I participate in full-contact origami. Years ago I discovered the meaning of life but forgot to write it down. I have made extraordinary four-course meals using only a mouli and a toaster oven. I breed prizewinning clams. I have won bullfights in San Juan, cliff-diving competitions in Sri Lanka, and spelling bees at the Kremlin. I have played Hamlet, I have performed open-heart surgery, and I have spoken with Elvis. But I have not yet gone to college."

Oh yes. I'd hire him. And be prepared to have to report to him, in no time.

To Get A Good Job...

In an application to Bates College, a hopeful future student wrote: "I have undergone many diverse activities in my life, and have eradicated meaning from every one."

•

Course Offerings

Last week, Teton County postal boxholders received course catalogs from Central Wyoming College, Jackson Community Education, the University of Wyoming, and the Art Association. Classes for adults and kids were offered in a variety of areas, from guitar playing to solar-electric power systems, to commercial law and art for all ages. You can learn a skill or earn a four-year degree in various curricula.

Included in the advertising supplements was an open letter to Teton County residents from Jim Fassler, the academic coordinator for the University of Wyoming. He asked that should anyone not find courses that interested him or her, to let him know. The implication was that perhaps somthing could be done to satisfy that concern.

Well, uh, Jim, there was one course I saw advertised a while ago in the bulletin for the New School for Social Research, Liberal Studies Division. It was "Time and Space in Modern Literature" and was described as:

> "a phenomenological inquiry into the spatiotemporal
> functions of human consciousness based on the premise
> that each person carries within himself a subjective
> time-system which helps him order and explain the
> amorphous experiences of self and world."

Heck, I might want to take that course myself. Depends on who's teaching it, naturally. A few courses listed in Teton County are certainly enticing. "Field Studies in Poetry Writing." "Fission, Fusion, and Psychosis." "Millennium." Good stuff, sure, but since you asked, there are a number of other offerings I'd like to see:

▸ Overcoming Peace of Mind
▸ Tax Shelters for the Indigent
▸ Under-Achievers Guide to
  Very Small Business Opportunities
▸ How You Can Convert
  Your Family Room
  Into a Garage
▸ Bio-Feedback and
  How to Stop It
▸ Tap Dance Your Way
  To Social Ridicule
▸ The Joys of Hypochondria
▸ Dealing with
  Post-Self-Realization Depression
▸ How to Overcome Self-Doubt
  Through Pretense and Ostentation
▸ Suicide and Your Health
▸ New Hope for the Dead

Adios, Monsieur Prufrock

Bird watching, my longtime hobby, has introduced me to many and varied topics and unexpected interests — as a good hobby should — and now, by devious means, to *The Love Song of J. Alfred Prufrock*, a poem by T.S. Eliot.

I'm pretty certain I would otherwise never have come to this particular poem. I come to poetry infrequently. Usually, I don't fully understand the genre. This Eliot piece is another one I don't entirely get — and in this I'm not alone, since a minor cottage industry has sprung up among English literature academics who even today come up with fresh, or perhaps reworked, interpretations of Prufrock's love song, written in the first part of the century.

A few bird watchers, writing about birds, somehow discovered Prufrock. In 1989 Robert Fisher reviewed his 40 years of bird watching, and asked, "Was it J. Alfred Prufrock who counted out his life in coffee spoons?" Fisher's query was taken from a line in the poem. At that time I simply assumed Prufrock was the guy who asked that, and abstractly wondered who he is, or was.

Now, in November 1996, comes Mel White, writing the lead article in a glossy birder's periodical, as follows:

"I have just about accepted, I think, the notion that I'm
never going to play first for the Yankees. (Although,
listen George Steinbrenner, if you're reading this, you
can contact me...) Likewise, the prospect that an audience
will rise as one to applaud my performance of the Hayden
Trumpet Concerto dims with each passing season — and it
was dim to the point of extinction even back when I
was practicing every day. It goes on, this list of brass rings
missed, growing longer as I plod into my Prufrockian

years and my sphere of possibilities shrinks like a leaky balloon."

Relating to Mr. White's set-up as I did initially, it was time to look up old J. Alfred—which I was able to do through the good offices of our wonderful county library and staff. It turns out that T.S. Eliot was writing about an unfortunate soul "frustrated by his poor self-image, his inadequate physical appearance, and his inability to speak to women."

He is a failure in the arena of male-female relationships. He cries out, "I should have been a pair of ragged claws, scuttling across the floors of silent seas."And he despairs, "I grow old...I grow old...I shall wear the bottoms of my trousers rolled."

Why, heck. That does it for me; no Prufrockian references shall appear in my ruminations henceforth. The poor guy was a loser.

•

The Gourmet Backpacker

When we first moved to Jackson the population numbered about 500. This was before multiplex movie theaters and focused television pictures; before innumerable events everyday of the year; before events got concocted that required semiformal wear and slippery shoes. It was a time winter nights—all 240 per year—mostly were without a scheduled event. Oh, you could go to a bar or the few restaurants that stayed open, to a church affair or private party. But there was little in the way of lectures, classes, courses, expert-led activities, group meetings, meetings to organize more meetings, meetings to find out what happened at the last meeting, and field trips to the first or last snaggletoothed violet of the season. It was a pleasant time marred only by an occasional case of cabin fever and a slightly elevated divorce rate.

One winter was particularly cold, with temperatures routinely bottomed out at –30, -40, -50 degrees. Inside our VW van that translated to –50, -60, -80 degrees, counting the wind chill. We didn't get out much.

In the middle of this notable winter an announcement appeared in the weekly newspaper inviting folks to a course in gourmet backpacking meals. Well! We hiked then. We ate on our hikes: soggy sandwiches, fruit, nuts and candy bars. Gourmet and backpacking didn't jibe: a classic oxymoron. That aside, an evening a week out of the house sounded great. We signed up.

And it was great. A warm place to be with compatible locals, an adequate number of bottles of wine, and gourmet food. Not food one could take or make on a backpacking venture, of course; there's seldom truth in advertising. But no one seemed to mind. Not when the menus included the following:

Smoked Trout/Truite Fumé by Yvon Chouinard
Marinade:

> 1/2 c. salt (no iodine)
> 1/3 c. brown sugar
> 1/3 c. soy sauce
> Juice of 1/2 lemon
> 1/2 tsp. black pepper
> 1 large clove garlic, chopped
> 1/2 tsp. seasoning salt
> 1 quart water
> Cut trout (9-12 depending on size) down the middle.

Butterfly; open to lay flat. Soak in marinade 4 hours in
a plastic, glass or stainless steel container.

Smoking:

Rinse marinated fish well in cold water. Pat dry with
paper towels and put on rocks of electric smoker. Smoke
with any hardwood, alder or willow. No bark.
Use three or four pans of wood.

To make jerky skin the fish and keep the smoker
door open two inches. After smoking, keep heat
on about 12 hours, or until dry. Store in plastic bag
or refrigerator.

Serve fish hot at the end of the smoking period.

I trust you picked up on the easy access to a dozen trout, an electric smoker, a refrigerator, lots of wood and oodles of time on your backpacking adventure. Other recipes called for simmering beans for 18 hours. Another for baked scallops in white wine required a pickup truck bed to carry all the pots, pans, wines, cheeses and fresh sea scallops, plus ingredients for minestrone alla Contadina and side dishes of rice, pasta and vegetables. (The recipe's originator, Anthony Parullo — a fine figure of a man — declared that hauling all that stuff to a park or backyard picnic bench was his idea of a backpacking venture.)

As for the matter of electricity to run a crockpot, electric smoker or refrigerator, the undaunted chefs suggested plugging into a current bush — an old joke that was definitely not a thigh-slapper.

To be completely honest about this adult course, I had to leave about three-quarters through the evening to teach a course of my own. A bird watching class. At night. In winter. At temperatures ranging from –20 to –45. Field study was rather a flop. The class was rather a flop. And I was never again asked to teach anything whatsoever in the adult education program.

P.S. The scallops in white wine dish is darn good, anywhere. If you can work it out on some hike or overnight, go for it.

A Study Has Shown...

Corn conversation

Investigators at one of the Department of Agriculture's experimental stations have been listening to what plants say when stressed by drought. Thus far, noise is all they've detected — very high frequency sounds, way up in the 100-kilohertz range. If a plant is getting sufficient water from its soil, the water and dissolved nutrients are drawn by capillary action up its water tubes. If soil is dry for an extended period, as in a drought, the water tubes fracture, emitting a high-pitched noise. (No *wonder* I've never caught a tree's response when I talk to it. I've probably never heard anything above 15 or 16 kilohertz. At best.)

What I can almost hear are comments made about some nutty research-type project to listen to plants talk. "What a waste of money!" "What good will it do?"

Assuming the researchers aren't just out-of-luck FBI guys with a no-win assignment, the impetus behind the investigation isn't to eavesdrop on the social life of geraniums, or listen to trees gossip; results may have numerous, far-reaching implications. One is that irrigators could monitor the sound of their crops, irrigating upon demand, with no waste of water or expense.

Other exciting prospects are: Using noise signals, can new varieties of plants be developed that are drought resistant? Do insects swarm to drought-stressed or diseased plants, guided by the plants distress noises, and, if so, can strategies for pest control be based on this phenomenon? Do bark beetles flock to trees sending off high frequency attractants? No telling what might come from this intriguing research.

Perhaps some researcher will ask what Meg and I want to know: "Did you hear what the willows whispered last night?"

•

Did Darwin have a dog?

More than once Stephen Jay Gould has started one of his columns in *Natural History* by noting that Charles Darwin and Abraham Lincoln were born on the same day in 1809. Obviously he considers it a real grabber. So do I: Dr. Gould is herewith granted permission to plagiarize one — one only — of my memorable beginnings. Which should amuse him there at Harvard.

But I digress.

One of Darwin's many theories, though certainly not his best known, is that non-human animals can learn to discriminate different human facial expressions. I suppose Chuck must have had pets, because any dog owner knows his pet recognizes that a smile is not a scowl and vice versa. The key phrase in Darwin's theory is that "can learn" part. It is believed that even human infants must learn how to recognize expressions; it is not innate.

At the University of Iowa, a Dr. Edward Wasserman is experimenting with pigeons. He has found they can be taught to recognize facial expressions, as well as assign photographs of objects in at least four categories: automobiles, flowers, cats and people.

Says Wasserman in a *New York Times* article, "Darwin raised the possibility of a continuity in mental development from animals to human beings, and it certainly looks as though he was right." (Wasserman's test results differ from others in this field of study, but I was taught to believe in a Wassermann test.)

His findings don't indicate that pigeons know what the human expressions mean. Yet once a pigeon learned to distinguish and categorize an expression, it could then accomplish the same categorization when looking at the faces of strangers, as well as photographs.

Steve Gould could write a learned essay on this, with historical references, personal interviews (of Wasserman; pigeons themselves say "No Comment") and the relationship between visual acuity and intelligence. Among other advantages, he has more assigned space.

I give you orts.

My eyesight isn't all that great, either.

•

Cold Fusion

Two months after Fleischmann and Pons publicized their claim to have demonstrated "electrochemically induced nuclear fusion," there was a workshop on Cold Fusion Phenomena. That was May 1989. In October 1989 there was a workshop on Anomalous Effects in Deutarated Materials, a distinct backing away from cold fusion. A physicist whom I shall not name wants still another workshop. He would call it Wildcat Drilling in the Physics Patch.

Some research don't get no respect.

•

Cold Fusion, Part II

The purpose of my experiment was, of course, to achieve cold fusion. The apparatus was appropriate: a battered old all-purpose metal cup; a generator out of a '51 Chevy, run off a 1/3 HP electric motor from a discarded washing machine; and a swizzle stick some honest-faced guy in a far-off place guaranteed me was pure titanium.

Materials: Two mutually soluble, clear, liquids with certain (proprietary) additives.

Control: Ice (How else to have "cold" fusion?)

Results: Despite observed generous gaseous evolution (which seemed to emanate, surprisingly, throughout the liquid body and not solely at the electrodes), no significant heat was found to evolve. Some ice did appear to melt, however, suggesting a so-far unexplained effect.

The experiment was inconclusive. I drank it.

To adhere to the scientific method — my credo, after all — I replicated the experiment. One needs a control. However, again no clear evidence of fusion could be detected, even with the most delicate instrumentation available. So I drank that one too. A third attempt also was inconclusive, although I did believe I could see something as I contemplated the mixture. But I didn't care any longer. Besides, I called a press conference and nobody came.

Conclusion: Cold Fusion results if one uses much ice when mixing together, say, tonic and gin. If I could only get a grant I'd like to expand this important work.

Cold Fusion: A tough job, but somebody has to do it.

Tree Reprieve

Investigators at the School of Earth and Atmospheric Sciences at Georgia Institute of Technology stated, back there in the go-make-'em-broke-80s, that natural hydrocarbons emitted by trees play a major role in creating ozone pollution in urban centers.

Researchers interested in the same kind of studies pointed out that the extension of the Georgia conclusion would be that if cities cut down all their trees and paved over their remaining vegetated areas why, Presto!, ozone levels would be significantly cut.

This was a problem for the GIT guys. Cities had already been relentlessly eliminating trees and burying all other plant life under concrete and macadam, yet ozone pollution hadn't been licked thereby.

The same GIT fellows went back to the drawing board and discovered that reducing the number of trees may, in fact, cause urban ambient temperatures to rise. Trees, they now declaim, provide natural air conditioning—because of the shade they provide and because of the cooling effect of evapotranspiration from their leaves. The chaps now conclude that ozone pollution control aimed at nitrogen oxide emissions from vehicles, power generation, etc., would likely be more effective than eliminating all trees.

Son of a gun.

•

The French Paradox

It's called the French Paradox in some journals and periodicals: Although French diets are high in saturated fat and cholesterol, the incidence of mortality from coronary heart disease is low. The French eat high on the hog—and then eat the hog—but they die of cardiac problems as if they ate rice, grains and a little peanut oil.

No one is sure why this is so—it's a paradox—but some investigators think it is linked to alcohol intake, particularly wine. High wine consumption has been shown to correlate with low coronary heart disease mortality in studies done in 17 countries. In fact, wine is the only substance besides dairy fat which shows a correlation with CHD. Wine appears to protect; dairy fat doesn't.

The answer to the paradox may be found in a phenolic compound that naturally occurs in grapes, scientifically labeled a *trans-resveratrol*. I really have no idea what it is—and insufficient interest to try to find out—but do know it is also found in grape leaves and kojo-kon, knotweed root used by Chinese and Japanese herbalists to treat "suppurative dermatitis, gonorrhea, favus, athlete's foot, hyperlipemia, arteriosclerosis and allergic and inflammatory diseases."

But you knew that.

Concentrations of trans-resveratol in reds tend to range higher than those found in white wine. Personally, I wish white wines were superior protectors. When I was just a wisp of a lad I over-indulged on a (cheap) red wine and have ever since had a mild psychoceramic reaction to reds.

Hmm. I wonder how much trans-resveratol is present in rot-gut gin...

•

Sperm

An analysis of 61 studies around the world concludes average human sperm counts have declined 42 percent in the past half century. The significant decline is not believed to be genetic, but caused by environmental factors. Persistent organic chemicals may pass from mother to fetus and cause lowered sperm counts, among other problems. Sperm counts are also affected by nutrition, socioeconomic status and stress.

Men are so sensitive.

In other work, a young doctoral student found that the act of making sperm seriously reduces the life span of a male worm, the nematode *Caenorhabditus elegans*. Male nematodes live far shorter than their mates. When their capacity to make sperm is eliminated — but their taste for intercourse is left intact by this decidedly clever investigator — they live at least 50 percent longer than normal, fertile males.

We're not just talking worms here, either. A scientist who studies this organism, Philip Anderson, says, "Those of us working with nematodes hold it as an article of faith that the genes and biochemical processes nematodes use are the same as those humans and other mammals use."

Less is bad.

So is more.

What's a guy to do?

•

It's not the heat, it's the stupidity

For several months I've been following, desultorily, an exchange of letters in an obscure journal. The general topic has been why — and I would add whether — it feels 10-15 degrees warmer in Idaho Falls, Idaho (elevation 4,300 feet), than it does at identical temperatures in Durham, North Carolina, elevation 400 feet. Conventional wisdom postulates because the air is drier in Idaho Falls, it feels warmer.

One writer scoffs at this idea. He has been arguing that the effect of humidity on the thermal properties of air and water vapor in each city is negligible. He theorizes that air density makes it feel warmer, because dense air is a better heat conductor. Air density is 15 percent less in Idaho Falls than it is in Durham as a result of the altitude difference; that translates to 17 percent less heat transfer at identical air temperatures. Lose less heat and you feel warmer. In English: It's not the humidity, it's the elevation.

Not so fast. Along comes a guy from Durham who suggests radiant heat transfer is also involved, that differences in daytime solar heating and nighttime heat loss in each situation result in large differences in surface temperatures. He proposes to conduct parallel measurements.

Isn't that always the way? Get a nice, simple explanation that flows trippingly off the tongue — "It's not the heat, its the humidity" — and somebody has to come along and get serious on you. Oh, well. Wait until the guy in Durham finds out that sometimes the ground surfaces around Idaho Falls are insulated in white, and on some nights heat radiates through clear, less dense air all the way to the beginning of the Big Bang. That may throw him.

Personally, whenever I've been some place where local wisdom has it that you won't feel hot at 100° because it's so dry, if it gets over 85° I'm flat hot.

As the cynics might have it: It ain't the heat, it's the stupidity.

•

Theory of Relativity

A new analysis of mysterious gamma-ray explosions in deep space, detected by the Compton Gamma Ray Observatory Spacecraft, indicates that the dimmer a short burst of intense energy is, the longer is its dura-tion—a phenomenon that lends new credence to time effects predicted by Einstein's theory of relativity.

I've been hearing about this or that finding that proves this or that corollary to 'ol Al's theory correct for a long time. Between us, I'm willing to accept all of it—the whole darn theory.

Don't you, honestly now, feel the same way?

•

Skip the raisins

A broadly knowledgeable friend has been telling us lately about the efficacy of gin-soaked raisins (nine per day) in easing arthritic pain. Now here's alternative medicine a person can get excited about...

Gin gets, or should get, its flavor, aroma and some of its essence from juniper berries. And, sure enough, *Potter's New Encyclopedia of Botanical Drugs and Preparations* says juniper acts as an anti-inflammatory.

In recent correspondence with *Chemical and Engineering News*, a Phil Lenz came to the same conclusion I reached a while back: If juniper is, in fact, the source of the active ingredient in a gin-raisin specific for arthritis, a person might want to simply skip the raisins.

•

Testosterone: Part 1

One of the shibboleths of the last half of this century is that too much testosterone makes a man aggressive. Hostile. Angry.

Well, X?*@!!..it may not be so. It may be too little testosterone does it. Wanna make something outta that?

Some miserable, weird researchers at the University of California found that a group of men with low testosterone levels were angry, irritable and aggressive until they were administered testosterone replacement therapy. Guess what? Their sense of anger decreased, and they became less irritable and aggressive. They were friendlier. Happier. More energetic.

Moreover, researchers elsewhere suggest that estrogen may contribute to male aggressiveness. (Males and females have both hormones.) Prepubescent females given estrogen become aggressive.

Natalie Angier, writing on this topic in the *New York Times* hinted it may be time for a new hormonal cliché to explain aggressiveness. She suggested this: "The estrogen was so thick you couldn't beat it down with a rolling pin."

That's irritating, don't you think?

•

Testosterone: Part 2

At the University of Oregon (Eugene), Dr. Jeri Janowsky found that older men given restorative doses of testosterone equal to hormone levels seen in 20-year-old men showed improvements in tests like mentally rotating a three dimensional object in space.

Just what they wanted, I bet.

•

Hear's to rock 'n roll

A couple of guys at Wilkes University in Wilkes-Barre, Pennsylvania, have discovered — to my enormous surprise — that auditory stimuli affects humans, in particular the human immune system.

Certain types of background music increase salivary levels of immuglobin A or IgA (not the stores). IgA plays a major role in fighting upper respiration infections such as colds, as well as indicating the overall health of immune system functions.

The IgA of people listening to Muzak — the innocuous, nondescript elevator stuff — rose 14.1 percent after 30 minutes. The IgA of a group listening to a random selection of soft jazz — wherever did they find that station? — rose 7.2 percent. People bathed in silence recorded a drop of less than one percent, statistically insignificant. Folks subjected to 30 minutes of alternating tone/click stimuli had a 19.7 percent IgA decrease.

I presume people subjected to 30 minutes of less-than-civilized, loud boom-boom noise featured on local radio stations went immediately into bronchitis, pneumonia and near-death experiences.

The Media

Press Excess

In my never-ending quest to bring you news of exciting and fresh events and occurrences, I attended a bash in Jackson thrown for the ministerial press—the press following our Secretary of State and the visiting Soviet Foreign Minister.

It was, to my unaccustomed eye, about a Grade III Roman Orgy, measured on the same scale as hurricanes. There were a few press guys there whose names or faces one might recognize; a lot of behind-the-scene press people who do various things (take pictures, write texts, go for stuff); locals handing out souvenirs, smiling at everything, making music, dancing, circulating, being seen; and a few out-of-place types, like me. Food, drink. Your standard bacchanalian feast.

I peeked into the press room (roomy, institutional) and the TV network rooms (full of monitors and aluminum cases), then moseyed. Chatted with a now big TV reporter I knew 20 years ago. He didn't remember me, of course; had this who-*is*-this-guy-look. Spoke with a CNN reporter, who had actually been to Russia. He quickly put on his who-is-this-guy look, and split. Spoke to some local; he put on his gee-if-he's-here-this-isn't-much-of-a-deal-as-I-thought-it'd-be-look.

Stimulated thereby, I searched all over for something to report. No ravens glowering down. No feathered thing whatsoever. There was a golden retriever for awhile, but he left.

Smart dog.

Eventually — and I'd have to say reluctantly — I noticed several young women swimming in the pool, parading around in bikinis and sunning themselves as though depravity, greed, jockeying for a new job, and an affected disdain for diplomacy were not rampant barely yards away.

I couldn't tell if they were press groupies, ordinary guests of the establishment determined to swim and acquire a tan, or foreign correspondents who hadn't seen sunshine lately. Since I was there to learn how the big time orgiasts do things, I ambled over to ask who they were. Power of the press, and all that.

One turned out to be a young woman trying her best to make peace on planet Earth. Gee. Has her own organization to promote peace, has been to Moscow, and will travel there again in a couple of months on a peace mission. Impressive; I bet only a few of those partying-down will ever make Moscow.

I was assured by an unimpeachable source—another much younger woman with her—that the peace lady was a body builder. She, indeed, had built a good bod, most of it on display, tanned to the color of the back pelage of a least weasel in summer. (Can't take the wildlife observer out of this party boy.)

Unhappily, just as she and I were getting down to the nuts and bolts—of her commitment, of course—the CNN guy and a serious-looking chap from Sweden zoomed in and my wildlife spotting faded to black.

I split.

Peace and friendship to all.

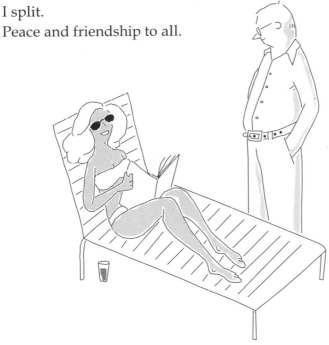

"Hmm," thinks the wily press guy. "Looks like the pelage of a fine least weasel."

What were they thinking?

The Tokyo Broadcasting System kicked in $12 million to send a TV reporter to the Soviet Mir space station for a week. All through the space race and thereafter earthbounds have complained that astronauts in space or on the moon describe every wonder their eyes behold as "fabulous," "incredible," or that old standard, "indescribable." If only, it is often said, a poet or writer could describe the sights and emotions. (This is often said by poets and writers.)

Well, heck, they should have known not to send a reporter. Especially a TV reporter. This guy gets up there and spends his communication time providing the details of space sickness and the particulars of ridding himself of his bodily wastes while in near-zero gravity. Entertaining stuff but, what with modern life and TV commercials, hardly educational or inspirational. His one experiment involved six tree frogs, and it flopped; the frogs went on a hunger strike. The fat frogs seemed to enjoy weightlessness, whereas the thin frogs just moped. This puzzled him; I understand completely.

Passing over his homeland the reporter mentioned the oceans off Japan looked polluted. What poetry.

The reporter was once his network's Washington bureau chief. Must be difficult to make these little adjustments.

•

TV Commercials

A few perceptive observers have pointed out that no longer must fellow citizens dash to their bathrooms, en masse, during commercial messages on TV. Commercial time has expanded so much that a person can take his time and easily make it back to the 12 minutes of programming wedged into endless advertising. A person can stroll, nibble on a piece of leftover pizza, make a couple of phone calls AND visit the necessary room.

It used to be that sewage treatment plant workers could correlate greatly increased flow from toilet use on the half and full hour marks. Hyped events—say a pro football game or congressional investigation—were recognized but on a less-regulated schedule.

Now, with more-or-less full-time commercials, they don't worry about flow surges unless OJ goes on a road trip or Seinfeld quits.

What a relief.

•

You Read It Here First

Once upon a time we lived in a community whose two newspapers (published daily and on Sunday, by golly) had influence on their readers. The papers would announce each Memorial Day that it was Spring!, and okay—if not mandatory—for everyone to get outside. Come Labor Day, editors warned their faithful readers that winter along the Great Lakes was here: Get inside.

We knew people who believed each of these silly pronouncements. One couple would bid "So long" to their neighbors and not emerge again—except in their car—until the newspapers gave absolution on Memorial Day.

Honest.

Newspapers, it seems to me, aren't that influential now. It's rumored they are on their way out. In fact, as of this pre-Memorial Day 1998 writing, some newspaper association or other is sponsoring advertisements urging parents to read newspapers to their kids. And for them to read newspapers. This public relations campaign is on TV.

Naturally.

•

It looks better on a dog

The Media. As they used to say about the mafia, "Who *are* those guys?" Television, for sure. Radio talk programs and PBS. C-Span. A few newspapers that have editorial policies. Magazines. Movies. Magazines. Movies. The internet. Lunch room chit-chat.

Probably all of the above, and more. Them's the media. We have been assured of late that various news media are mostly liberal.

Right. I don't believe that for a New York minute. Meg and I read a fair selection of newspapers and news magazines. We watch well-known TV programs and converse about public affairs. If most of the talking heads, editorial writers, commentators and columnists are left-wing zealots, they sure have us hoodwinked.

In nineteen hundred and ninety-eight America's president, William Jefferson Clinton, is under unprecedented scrutiny with respect to his personal life and character. Why don't we question the character of the scrutineers? I can't name a half dozen media types who don't slobber to repeat each and every lurid suggestion, innuendo and unsubstantiated allegation antagonistic to Clinton.

But why just pick on Clinton? The media are Pavlovian in their response to any item considered newsworthy. Throw in scandal, murder, sex or celebrity involvement—however distant—and salivating commences.

Ernie Kovacs said it about TV, but it holds true for the rest of the pack: TV is called a medium because it's neither raw nor well done.

In the News

Is Your Doctor a Space Alien?

My ol' doc, brandishing a spleen-sized belt buckle, urges me to issue a medical alert. Certainly. Always glad to help in such matters.

A writer for the *Weekly World News* interviewed a Terrence Starnes, identified as a leading UFO expert. Starnes claims that thousands of space aliens are masquerading as medical doctors in America. "These extraterrestrial impostors have infiltrated the medical establishment...to achieve their evil ends."

Well, bless Bess. I had no idea.

Starnes goes on to declaim that "medical authorities are aware of the situation and have actually conspired to keep it under wraps to avoid a public relations nightmare."

As to a public service, then, here's a partial listing of how to know if your doctor is a space alien:

- Beware of doctors who have trouble identifying body parts.
- Human physicians often run late, forcing people to wait hours to see them. Aliens are on time.
- A human doctor's handwriting is usually quite sloppy. Extraterrestrials generally labor over their writing, making it the easiest-to-read printing you'll ever find.
- Legitimate doctors display their original medical license and medical school diploma prominently on their walls. Blank walls, photocopied licenses or diplomas from schools you've never heard of strongly suggest something is wrong.

- New magazines in the waiting room. This is an alien concept.
- Most doctors draw blood for testing but need very little to get the job done. Physicians who ask for a quart of blood clearly have a hidden agenda — and may be extraterrestrials.

"Take these signs seriously," warns our own unidentifiable fried objects expert. "If two or more of these apply to your doctor, he/she is almost certainly a space alien."

My ol' doc is about a one and three-quarters.

•

Galileo Was Right

Pope John Paul II has put right a wrong the Church made in 1633 when it condemned Galileo for having proved Earth isn't the center of the solar system, but moves around the Sun. Galileo was forced by the inquisition to either recant or be burned at the stake.

Galileo publicly recanted his findings as "abjured, cursed and detested" and settled for house arrest. He was, after all, not a dummy.

He was not the first to understand that the Earth orbits the Sun. Ptolemy made this correct observation in the second century. In 1543 Copernicus published Ptolemy's theory. But when, in 1632, Galileo published actual discoveries made with an astronomical telescope he himself built — confirming Ptolemy's theory — it was too much.

Over a hundred years later, in 1755, the Roman Catholic Church removed its ban on Galileo's "Dialogue Concerning the Two Chief World Systems." Two hundred twenty-four years (but who's counting) passed before a panel of theologians, historians and scientists convened in 1979 to examine the 1633 condemnation. It only took the panel five years to make its preliminary report, indicating Galileo had been correct. Eight years later, in 1992, Pope John Paul II formally acknowledged the Church had been in error.

Sometimes its hard to keep matters to a tight agenda.

•

Sexual Harassment

The U.S. Navy has come up with a one-page, bulletin board instruction sheet to define (and one wishes to presume, reduce) sexual harassment. It used traffic light colors to identify appropriate and inappropriate behavior between the sexes.

The admiral responsible for the definition says that since "we're in a communications age, with a sound-bite, bumper sticker mentality, we're looking for something to get young people's attention." (One presumes even the admiral couldn't explain away the oxymoron implicit in that rationalization.) Examples from the notice:

▸ Green - Go: A polite compliment or everyday social interaction. "Hello, how are you?"
▸ Yellow - Slow Down to Stop : Getting sexual or gesturing sexually, leering or staring.
▸ Red - Stop: Grabbing, forced kissing. Rape.

Gee, if this simple definition method of communicating even kind of works, it could be expanded:

▸ Previously Owned: Check for wear-and-tear.
▸ Take the Bus: Un-American

- ▸ Reconditioned: Not for long trips.
- ▸ Good only for parts: Worn-out.
- ▸ Cherry: Obsolete term.
- ▸ Needs engine rehaul: Check repair record.
- ▸ Antique: Use only in parades.
- ▸ Valley Car: A waste of money.

•

Sold, to the highest bidder

Frenzied and largely unseemly bidding in New York last week for articles once belonging to Jackie Kennedy Onassis reminded me that I have some coins once carried by Jack Kennedy.

Oh, to be sure, it was before he became president. Presidents and senators seldom carry cash or wallets — let alone keys — because those things make pockets bulge, and bulging pockets don't photograph well. Regardless, these coins slipped out of Mr. Kennedy's pocket into the tucked seam of a squishy armchair in a room in the Madison Hotel in Washington, D.C.

I shall never reveal the room number, nor the actual day on which this occurred.

These coins come to only $1.37, and they're in a plain brown paper bag. Moreover, there is no substantiation whatever that any of the above is factual. (Well, except for my reputation for accurate reportage.)

Notwithstanding all that, after learning of the Onassis auction, I will part with these Kennedy coins, on the Q.T., for a mere $950.

A great deal. Sotheby's would probably get a couple of thou, easy, then take a big percentage on top of that.

First come, first served.

Food Safety

If you're reading this it's safe to assume you outwitted foodborne pathogens, contaminants and micro-organisms to survive another Thanksgiving.

Not that food safety isn't a serious matter. It is. In the United States alone, salmonella infects a minimum of 800,000 people each year. This bacterial poisoning can cause diarrhea, reactive arthritis, systemic infections and death.

Camplyobacter, found in raw or undercooked chicken, unpasteurized milk and untreated water, causes acute infectious diarrhea and death. Two to four million cases occur each year, causing 120 to 360 fatalities.

Escherichia coli is responsible for 23,000 cases of foodborne illness that lead to some 100 deaths annually. Vibrio, found in seafood, kills half of those it infects, many of whom already have underlying illnesses.

The above are bacteria. Two protozoa are also serious pathogens. *Toxoplasma gondii* is found in raw or undercooked meat, unwashed fruits and vegetables, and cat feces. Symptoms of infection may range from none or slight to mental retardation and death. Approximately 1.4 million cases and 300-plus deaths occur each year. It may kill or cause birth defects in fetuses.

Cryproporidium parvum made the news in 1993 when it flourished in a batch of fresh apple cider. It played havoc with Milwaukee, Wisconsin's water supply the same year, sickening over 400,000 people.

Don't forget viruses. Norwalk virus affects 200,000 people annually. In the news lately are illness reports associated with Norwalk found in oysters contaminated with sewage. Hepatitis A symptoms include fever, nausea, abdominal discomfort, jaundice and death. Only five percent of reported Hepatitis A cases in the United States are believed to be due to food (although tainted strawberries sold to a school lunch program led to a 1997 outbreak). Most cases result from person-to-person fecal-oral contact.

There are other microbial pathogens slinking around, waiting for a host to appear — but enough.

I wonder how those Pilgrims and Indians managed, what with no little plastic buttons bred into those wild turkeys, no meat thermometer, no running water, and veggies fertilized by who-knows-what-means.

•

Squirrel Brains

In the past four years, 11 cases of a human form of transmissible spongiform encephalopathy — called Cruetzfeldt-Jacobs disease — have been diagnosed in rural western Kentucky. Six of the 11 have died; every one of them were squirrel-brain eaters.

Squirrels are a popular food item in rural Kentucky, where people eat either the meat or the brains, but generally not both. Those who eat squirrel brains prepare them one of two ways: In the first, the fur is shaved off the top of the head and the head is fried whole. The skull is then cracked open at the dinner table and the brains sucked out. Alternately, an uncooked skull is cracked open and the brains are scooped out, then scrambled with white gravy or eggs.

Those families who eat only squirrel meat carcasses from the hunt or from road kill prepare the meat with vegetables in a stew called "burgoo."

The clinical director of the Neurobehavorial Institute in Hartford, Ky., where the Kentucky squirrel-brain eaters were treated, noted that while his patients theoretically could have contracted the disease from other sources, such as beef, there has not been a single confirmed case of mad cow disease in the U.S.

And, he allowed, since every one of the 11 people with the disease ate squirrel brains, it seems prudent for people to avoid this practice.

Not a problem.

•

Let Sleeping Bears Lie

A female black bear, interviewed as she prepared to leave her winter den, admitted Special Prosecutor Kenneth Starr had issued her a subpoena. The encounter allegedly occurred several years ago when President Clinton vacationed in Jackson Hole and camped overnight in Grand Teton National Park. Any sexual contact, which the president denies, was or would have been consensual. No long-term relationship claims have been made by either party.

Unique aspects of the bear's pending testimony include interspecies contact, and a potential witness, viz. a great horned owl, whose precise location is under investigation.

The sow just emerged from hibernation. Groggy but awake enough to realize the implications of her subpoena, she refused further comment, citing advice of counsel. This reporter has learned, however, that she has yet to retain counsel. Pressed for comment, the bruin remarked that a good lawyer willing to accept futures in huckleberry bushes is hard to find. So is finding a good lawyer. All she knows is that she's still sleepy, very hungry, and is being pestered by two cubs she didn't know she had had.

Critics of the president are, of course, shocked, and are considering articles of impeachment.

And Justice For All

Animal, Vegetable, Mineral

Some weeks ago — oh, maybe a month; time flies — the U.S. Supreme Court decided that the tomato is a vegetable. I didn't follow the case or the arguments, let alone the basis or need for the court to involve itself in this matter.

Who knew? It's all rather surprising about the tomato.

Now I learn that rats, mice and birds are declared not to be animals. This comes from the U.S. Department of Agriculture under its reading of

Some of my best friends are vegetables. Really.

Hey, at least you're not ketchup.

Non-animals offer comfort to Tommy Tomato. A vegetable.

the Animal Welfare Act, which regulates treatment of laboratory animals. It turns out rats, mice and birds haven't been animals since 1971, when the act went into effect. Sure slipped past me.

I guess it slipped past the Humane Society, too. Just two years ago, it and the Animal Legal Defense Fund sued to have these creatures redefined. Made animals again, don't you see. A U.S. District Court judge ruled the USDA had been "arbitrary and capricious" in excluding them from the animal kingdom.

The USDA appealed.

Now the U.S. Court of Appeals has decided — on a technicality — in favor of the USDA. (Technicalities can be bothersome, yes?) This technicality was that the Humane Society and the Animal Legal Defense Fund had no legal standing to sue initially, because they were not directly injured by the USDA determination.

There will be an appeal to a still higher court.

I wonder what the implications are for a rat or a mouse or a bird to be a laboratory non-animal, or for a tomato to be a vegetable and not a fruit.

There are days when I wish the court would annul or mitigate gravity. This is one of those.

•

No SIN in Cincinnati

There is no SIN in Cincinnati, so the slogan goes. (Doesn't have to be; Kentucky is just across the river.) Prosecutors there tried to prove to a jury of eight that seven of 175 photographs shown at the Contemporary Arts Center last Spring were obscene.

Prospective jurors were asked whether they collected art, whether they had ever attended an art class, or for what purpose they ever went to a museum. More succinctly, "Why did you have cause to visit an art museum; was it for a field trip?" (Get real, sir. Why *else* would anyone ever enter a museum?)

Seven of the resulting jury were from the most conservative suburbs of lesser Cincinnati...the ones, one supposes, up in those seven hills away from the river. Yet, in the end, the museum was found not guilty. There had been no sin in Cincy.

Ah, but there was one woman who said, on questioning, that she didn't think she should serve on the jury. Said she, "Because of my moral and Christian beliefs, I don't think I can be fair."

Sometime slogans go out of style.

•

Our hero

A James Brown was in the papers last week with the doggondest quote. I never heard the like; I've led such a sheltered life. Mr. Brown said he "*set an example* for the nation by not fighting the criminal charges" that landed him in prison. Said he didn't contest the charges because, "being a hero and a legend like Martin Luther King, it would have been detrimental to the community, and it would have just ruined this country!" (There was no exclamation point, but one might be assumed.) Said Brown, "It was a sacrifice. I'm like Kennedy — it's not what your country can do for you, it's what you can do for your country."

Well, I never.

Can't help wondering who James Brown is, and what he did to get imprisoned, and what, indeed, he does. If a guy has saved the United States from ruination, I'd like to know a wee bit about him. Since he's a hero and everything.

Thanks, Brown. Appreciate it. Who the heck are you?

•

Jim Bakker and Zsa Zsa

Taking precedence in the nightly news are two nagging questions: "Is Jim Bakker's sentence appropriate for his massive tele-evangelist frauds?" And, "Was Zsa Zsa fairly punished for her offense?" Zsa Zsa, you will recall, was uncooperative with officers who pulled her over for a traffic violation. Seems sentencing has become a matter for a public poll to determine.

I'm not an instant expert on criminal justice so I don't know about Bakker's sentence. However, 10 years before a chance for parole doesn't sound out of line. But poor Zsa Zsa. Her lawyer stands up before cameras and says she's *too old* for jail time. The judge sentences her to put her *real age* on her next driver's license.

As we used to hear during the Watergate and Iran-Contra days, she has suffered enough. Too old; horrors. Surely cruel and unusual punishment.

Free Zsa Zsa.

•

Savages

Two Tlingit youths, boys or young men as you will, got into trouble and were caught. These Alaskan citizens of an American Indian tribe robbed and severely beat a man in Washington state. Tribal elders sought and won court permission to administer appropriate justice. They plan to exile each 17-year-old to a separate, isolated and uninhabited island for up to two years, where each will have to survive on his own, or die. Really finding themselves, not just a T-shirt motto. Beyond that, the Tlingits—acting as a society, a family—will make restitution to the victim. It's part of their culture, not to say civilization.

Why, those savages. There they go again. I sure hope that recognizing the individual's anti-social behavior and criminal activity—and acknowledging society's role in developing morals and codes of behavior—doesn't catch on.

It would mess up the ways of the White Eyes.

•

Done in by laundry

The person currently receiving the most media attention in Washington, D.C., is Draco. Why, it's a "Draconian proposal" here, a "Draconian measure" there, a "Draconian speech" being given, a "Draconian idea" yet to be revealed. Only the TV interviews are missing.

One isn't scheduled: Draco isn't available for comment. Draco was chief magistrate of Athens in the 7th century. He and a majority of fellow legislators systematized the laws of city-state Athens, establishing what became known as Draco's code.

In a memorable article in the *New York Times*, reporter David Rosenbaum wrote that under Draco's code, "the penalty for every infraction, from vagrancy to murder, was death.

"Draco once explained the lack of gradations in his punishments by saying that, hard as he tried, he couldn't think of tougher penalties."

A generation later, the legislature transferred power to Solon to reform the state, which under Draco was experiencing huge social unrest. Solon—a legislator, poet and intellectual—repealed most of Draco's laws. He gave political influence to the lowest classes of Athenians and established a legitimate judicial system.

Draco still had his fans. Law-and-order citizens amongst those gathered for a play rose, cheered, and threw their clothing on Draco when he entered the theater, a then-popular gesture of approval and approbation. Draco smothered under the pile.

It was probably an accident.

But one wonders what punishment was meted out to members of the crowd.

And whether the show went on.

Rascals, Politicians & Bureaucrats

A letter to the folks

Dear Aunt Taxpayer and Cousin Citizen,

The other Monday we went out into the field to attend the rededication of Jackson Lake Dam. (Sure, we were invited; we don't gate crash.) I guess this was the second rededication; the first dam washed out before your time.

Anyway, a little while back, after the Teton Dam collapsed in Idaho, people around here got to wondering about the safety of the Jackson Dam, and they worked their fret into a rebuild, fix-em-up modification program. This time Jackson Lake Dam is supposed to be good against a 100-year earthquake or 7.5 on Professor Richter's scale, whichever comes first.

They had a real nice day for the ceremony. Good crowd. More stand-ups than sit-downs, but we were led to chairs. That was nice. The lake is pretty, and pretty darn full. Never saw more water in it.

There were big shots all over. Local Idaho and Wyoming big shots mostly wore sporty cotton jackets, caps with those holes in back, and boots. Flatlander big shots wore suit jackets and slippery shoes and carried brief-cases.

Matter of fact, one guy's briefcase sat on one of those chairs through-out the entire deal. Nobody dared move it and sit down. I guess it belonged to the kind of guy who follows presidents these days, with the losing com-bination in the black satchel. Maybe this bag had the secret of how to make the dam gates work properly.

There was this little bitty platform perched out over the edge of the dam face and I know a couple of the people sitting on it were wondering if it was put together by the contractor. At least one guy hoped it wasn't.

Then a local Cub Scout troop presented the colors and led the pledge of allegiance. That was cute. I hadn't heard much about the pledge since the last election. By gosh, it's still around and seems okay.

Then they got down to speech-making and back-patting. Cousin, there was more back-slapping than you'll see in a pro football game. With overtime. Everybody congratulated everybody. The Bureau of Reclama-tion itself, the NPS, Forest Service, the contractor, the politicians, the irriga-tors, and who-all.

Despite comments made by the "Instant Experts," Jackson Lake Dam is completely... um... safe.

Then the contractors congratulated themselves and everybody. And then the irrigators — well, you can see how it went.

Auntie, I don't recall that the taxpayers and ordinary citizens ever got mentioned, let alone thanked or congratulated. Of course, what with all the speeches and the sun and the clouds, I may have nodded off now and again. But I don't think so.

I do remember one speaker talking about "Instant Experts." He congratulated all the Bureau folks and the contractor and everybody for their forbearance and courtesy and for not getting bent out-of-shape when what he called Instant Experts dared to speak out at public meetings about this dam work. So I guess he meant Instant Experts are people who attend public meetings where public input is requested and even required by law and, by George, say what's on their minds.

What is this republic coming to?

But then a couple of cooler heads, while they didn't exactly embrace public input, allowed that possibly some good might have come from it, and moreover they're all going to have to live with that environment stuff.

Well, Cuz, I guess they will. It's in the law now. And anyhow people who had fought doing this or that good deed were right there getting their backs slapped and applause for having done this or that.

It was a caution folks, a pure caution.

Oh, right there at the end of the festivities they announced that the dam was working just fine now. (There was some snickering at that in the audience, but maybe they were just simply getting into the spirit of the occasion.) I was glad to hear that, because the river seems real warm down where we all used to fish, like it was coming from the reservoir surface. And the lake really is pretty darn high. And over by the gates was a group of guys with hard hats on their heads and looks of panic on their faces.

Then we went over to a shady spot and had cookies and punch and that was real nice. Wish you had been there. Best regards.

P.S. Found out the gates were stuck. They were repaired at 2 a.m. the next morning.

•

Ten Billion Trees

President Bush proposed the planting of a billion trees in each of the next 10 years. Ten billion trees by 2000. (Better known as The Year Two Thousand.) Ten billion trees should absorb perhaps 13 million tons of carbon dioxide a year, about five percent of the U.S.'s current emissions of CO_2.

There's even an Earth Corps proposal, a kind of amalgamation of the Peace Corps and the Civilian Conservation Corps but under a non-profit private corporation aegis. All most commendable, sensible. It would be nice to have the goal of 10 billion trees exceeded. Trees are nice.

Right here at the people's White House, history says, presidents once went out and directed the planting of trees their own selves. Put a mulberry tree there, said Tommy Jefferson, and there, directed Teddy. And plant a shrub over yonder, declared Franklin. Lady Bird reveled in flowers. (I don't count Ike's putting greens and the infamous tennis courts.) Back in those long-gone days a president would look around and put a walnut or elm or whatever where he wanted it.

Imagine the scenario today. First, polls would have to be taken— and found unqualifiedly positive. If not, the spin doctors would be called in to alter public opinion. A blue-blood committee would be formed and

71

given 90 to 180 days to come up with a list of trees most favored by voters in all categories. (Well, not liberals. Get real.) The National Security Council would be called into session and asked for comment. The Secret Service would have to assess potential dangers, from allergies to obstructing branches.

Marine Corps helicopter pilots would conduct tests on various tree species for arboreal resistance to down-drafts. Administration spokespersons would judge photo opportunity propensities, lighting angles, and general ambiance. Communications people would decide whether use of various devices — such as cellular phones and hand-and-ear held radios — would be impaired by some fool tree.

An environmental impact statement would be issued so public input could be ignored. The Environmental Protection Agency would issue bulletins on trees and shrubs, and environmental groups would be urged to get behind the president on this one.

The Agriculture Department would commence a search for healthy specimens, inspecting the saplings for insect pests. (If bugs are found, EPA officials would permit emergency use of some banned pesticide, to be applied somewhere out of sight.) The Department of Commerce would clear any interstate trucking needed. Interior would supply a special engraved and silver-plated shovel, unfortunately going through the Pentagon's purchasing system to buy it. Daniel Quayle would be put in charge of drip irrigation. Orders would be issued, approved by Sununu, changed by Sununu and ignored by the gardeners. And one fine day — at the wrong season for the particular tree species chosen — some wilted and dried-out sapling or shrub would be stuck into the ground.

At least a good supply of fertilizer is available in the immediate vicinity.

Thanks, Mr. Budget guy

Politicians like to focus on some goal down the road when they don't have to deal with it. Today's problems, after all, are so bothersome. Take this global warming thing. How much easier to send a memo to everyone in the Executive Branch urging that the best tactic is to adopt an approach that raises "the many uncertainties." To crank up the speech writers and send some guy out to speechify thusly: "Americans did not fight and win the wars of the 20th Century to make this world safe for green vegetables."

Thank you for that, Mr. Budget Director. Next time stick to budget thaumaturgy.

•

The New Forestry

A group of scientists in the Pacific Northwest has found that the conventionally held notion of clear-cutting a forest — followed by controlled burns or herbicide application to prepare the site for agri-trees — may, in fact, not allow regenerating woodlands effectively to utilize nutrients, and reduces their resistance to pests. To say nothing of increasing soil erosion.

These chaps also found that fallen logs and forest debris are vital to organisms and animals, which in turn are vital to processing nutrients and returning them effectively to the soil. They found that standing trees left in a timbered area provide habitat for remaining plants and animals, as well as shade and cover.

Aren't you surprised?

According to Dr. Jerry Franklin of the University of Washington, instead of being a waste and fire hazard — as the U.S. Forest Service considered them in their advocacy of clear-cutting—standing trees, fallen logs, forest litter and timbering debris are capable of doing great good. To quote the good doctor, "In retrospect, it's almost unbelievable that we could have been that stupid."

I like a guy with the gift of droll understatement.

•

Why didn't I think of that?

When candidate George Bush was running as the "environmental president," he declaimed that, if elected, his administration would see to it that in the future there would be "no net loss of wetlands" in our country. In office, by golly, his administration promulgated rules to guide and establish the uses to which bottomlands, low-lying areas, riparian lands, marshes, forests and seasonally wet areas can be put to ensure their long-range protection.

Fast forward to the next election campaign. I can almost hear the strategy meeting: "Keep the environmental president thing, but see what can be done about releasing some of that wimpy wetland stuff for use. Let's see now, What can we do? Wait, I got it!..."

The Bush Administration is proposing a new definition of "wetland." The effect of the new definition would be to remove protection from tens of millions of acres of, um, previously wet lands.

The present definition was set by a committee of technicians and scientists from the Environmental Protection Agency, the Department of the Interior, and the Army Corps of Engineers.

The proposed new definition of wetlands was made—according to a recent article in the *Washington Post*—by the White House Council on

Competitiveness, a six member group of administration officials headed by the vice president. The council is guided by industrial, building and agricultural interest groups.

It must have been a helluva close call.

Kind of puts me in mind of the time when a former colleague who moved to Los Angeles called to report that the smog problem there had been dramatically reduced in severity. Seems the pollution control people simply changed their definition to read that human tolerance for smog was three times greater than it had been yesterday.

What elegance. Simplicity itself. Just raise the parts per million acceptable level a few fold, and magically there are hardly any days when Los Angeles isn't within "acceptable levels of pollution." My colleague chided me for all that fussing around with other potential solutions. I apologized; never occurred to me.

Directly affected, should this new approach to "protection" of wetlands be approved, will be breeding grounds for ducks, other birds and fish. Resting areas for geese. Plant habitat and natural storm control systems—at least according to the existing regulations.

The White House spokesperson's new, flippant definition goes: "Not every puddle is a wetland."

Yes, of course. And not every pledge is honored.

•

The zeros in government

Sometimes I ponder whether presidential hopefuls Dole, Gingrich, Perot, Dornan, Robertson, etc., etc., etc., have even the slightest notion of what they're saying when they yak about the national budget, national deficit, national debt and the nation's economy.

To be charitable, maybe it's because the numbers are so enormous. To be less charitable, perhaps it harks back to when I was a lad, when there was a mordant joke that when millionaires call for sacrifice, the poor tremble.

A million is a concept that people I know comprehend; the notion of a single person becoming a billionaire is inconceivable. The idea of a nation messing around with a trillion dollar economy — let alone a $4.4 trillion debt — is surely beyond everyone's imagination, sort of like grasping the concept of "light year. "

Follow me here. A million is a thousand thousands: 1,000,000. Well, sure. A billion is a thousand millions: 1,000,000,000. Huh? A trillion is a thousand billions: 1,000,000,000,000. (The English cleverly say it aloud, a thousand billions. Good show.) But what does it mean? John Paulos, in his recent book on what he calls "innumeracy," put it this way:

It takes 11 1/2 days for a million seconds to tick away.

To takes 32 years for a billion seconds to pass.

It takes 32,000 years — thirty-two thousand! — for a trillion seconds to pass.

Well, heck. That helps me — particularly when some pol stands in the well and drawls out some phrase like $27,000, then in the next breath blithely skips over $650 billion.

•

Smart Move

To my certain knowledge, Sen. Malcolm Wallop, R-Wyo., was a birdwatcher and probably still is. He used to participate in Christmas Bird counts in northeastern Wyoming. Maybe still does.

The *Jackson Hole Daily* of September 22, 1994, carried the news that

Sen. Wallop succeeded in getting Wyoming and Idaho dropped from the proposed Old Faithful Protection Act, designed to protect Yellowstone National Park's thermal features from threats beyond the park's boundaries. Sen. Wallop offered an amendment to the Senate Energy Committee to drop both Wyoming and Idaho from the bill in his apparent belief that those states don't pose any threat to Yellowstone. At least in this regard.

His amendment passed in committee, 11-9. For shame.

In July 1994, Sen. Wallop proposed eliminating five national parks and five national wildlife refuges. Why, he even proposed one of those expensive studies to that end.

In May 1994, Malcolm Wallop spoke to the Senate and, referring to his announcement not to run for re-election, stated it was "the wisest decision of my political career."

Could be.

•

The Law of Unintended Results

It's unbelievable how some politicians, pundits and talking microphones propagandize what messages we Americans intended by our vote in last November's elections.

It goes like this: "Last November the American people sent a message..." and continues with their own cynical interpretation of what we supported by casting our ballots.

I didn't vote to prevent or delay the Department of Agriculture from establishing higher standards for meat and poultry inspections. Did you? Did you send a message that scientific testing for dangerous bacteria should not be done? Is that why you went to the polls?

Did you mean to say that the Environmental Protection Agency should not be instructed to implement water quality standards in the Great Lakes? As a patriotic American, do you actually desire to see 20 percent of the Earth's fresh water polluted?

Will you be happier, more productive and have improved family values if San Diego is granted permanent exemption from the Clean Water Act's requirement that the city purify its sewage before dumping it into the Pacific Ocean?

Did you request that public lands be sold off? Really? Seems to me no-entry signs, security fences and discouragement of innocent travel immediately follow the transfer of land to private hands.

Did you telegraph that you wish cancer-causing chemicals to show up in processed foods? Or to exempt industry from responsibility for hazardous wastes they dumped because they dumped them before the Superfund law, making you pay for the clean-up?

Have you faxed anyone to cut off research into mine safety or to resume off-shore drilling in ecologically sensitive areas? Was it your fax that urged dirtier air, contaminated public water supplies and higher levels of toxic wastes in rivers and lakes?

It's something, isn't it? You went and voted out of a sense of responsibility — or to vote a rascal out — only to install a new one. Or because you thought it was "time for a change," only to be astonished at the change. Or — heaven forbid — because the candidate met your idea of a congenial, good-looking person.

Well, I voted last November. Here's my message: I don't support balancing the national budget by throwing away the last four decades' efforts to control pollution and clean up our nation. Or by becoming uncompassionate towards the less fortunate in our society. Or by attacking the arts and humanities. Or by cutting research. Or by selling off our land and delivering to succeeding generations — those children so often referred to — a country wrecked beyond recovery.

I did not vote for that course.

•

Big Al, the People's Pal

Sen. Alan Simpson, R-Wyo., recently stated that "some environmentalists bring ridicule upon themselves, and the best way to defeat them is with ridicule." I hope his operative word in that quotation is "some," as in some lawyers, some writers, some baseball players and, yes, even some senators.

It occurs to me that attempts to defeat environmentalists have relied almost exclusively, for many decades, on ridiculing individuals as opposed to evaluation of the facts. Perhaps it's because refutation of environmental positions is usually not possible.

•

Scandal

This year marks the 75th anniversary of the Teapot Dome investigation. The scandal concerned oil reserves at Teapot Dome in Wyoming and Elk Hills, California, which were transferred from the Navy to the Department of Interior by President Harding.

Subsequently, Albert Fall, then head of Interior, leased the Teapot Dome fields, without competitive bidding, to oil operator Harry Sinclair.

Similarly, the Elk Fields field was leased without competition to Edward Doheny.

The senate investigation into the matter discovered that Doheny had lent Fall $100,000 interest-free, and that Sinclair also had "loaned" Fall a large sum. Fall was convicted of accepting bribes and went to prison for a year.

Doheny and Sinclair were acquitted, but Sinclair later went to jail for contempt of the Senate and for hiring private investigators to shadow members of the jury considering his trial.

Ah, the good old days.

•

Sinister Force

Earlier this month Congress learned that a bill it recently passed contained a provision that created a windfall for the tobacco industry — a little matter of some $50 billion.

No one noticed it during the debate and vote, a circumstance probably not all that unusual in Congress; it is to be doubted that when any member votes on a particular measure he or she fully comprehends each nuance contained within. There are lots and lots of words written by experts in obfuscation — volumes of words competing against pressure of time, obligations, schedules and vacations. Busy, busy, busy.

What is surprising is that no one seems to know how that provision ever got into the bill. Not a single congressmen owns up to sponsoring the provision. No staffer or congressional aide confesses to have slipped it in, perhaps after hours. Somehow, it magically got into the bill and was voted upon.

As Al Haig once said—in connection with a mysterious 18 1/2-minute gap in an audio tape, it had to have been a "sinister force" operating after hours in the hallowed halls of Congress. There must have been another sinister force operating this time.

What else could it be?

•

Yo, Saddam!

Saddam Hussein must be the worst signal reader since Scarlett believed Rhett would yield once more to her charms. Maybe since variances began getting added to the Commandments.

Why, every time our president, secretaries of this or that post, U.N. diplomats, military big-wigs or leaders of many lands speak out on the Persian Gulf, they each and every one say they're sending "signals." There's a half-million military men and women with planes and ships and tanks and who knows what all gearing up for war just out of Hussein's sight. There's global TV and personality interviews and missions of all kinds, sending their clear, clarion signals to Saddam. Who apparently isn't getting them.

My own decoding of the signals is scrambled, too, come to that. Something critical is missing, leading me to conclude there must be more to this frenetic diplomatic and military activity than we've been told—some overwhelming reason to take Saddam off the world scene. And now. But then, why go into heavily defended Kuwait? Why not Baghdad?

Perhaps the wrong signals are being sent to both Saddam and the American people.

Campaigning

Word control

Columns in newspapers, magazines and journals perform public service. Certainly they do; just reflect upon this series, for starters. So, as authorized by the highly regarded but variable organization—Columnists, Recent and Past (acronym deleted)—I offer advice to all my fellow citizens currently vying for public office. (I start with the assumption, naturally, that each of them has only sincere and unreserved desire to serve his fellows and perform civil service in its pure, honorable and unselfish ideal.)

The suggestions below are not my inspiration; I am indebted for them to a group called Gopac, which uses focus groups to draw its recommendations. Gopac advises candidates it favors to call their political opponents, "sick, pathetic, liberal, incompetent and tax-spending traitors."

Ah, but call yourselves, you hopeful servants-to-be of this great republic, "humane, visionary, candid, confident and hard working reformers."

I guess "honest" might not play in Peoria this year.

A caveat was subsequently added to refute "traitor." Apparently, other Gopac focus groups found the term to reflect poorly upon the utterer and not the opposition. Be careful of that word.

Removing "traitor" reduced the recommended total of good and bad words to 132. Not to worry: It's still acceptable to call your opponent "corrupt, bizarre or permissive," and to pride yourself on being "courageous, principled, caring, and pioneering." Not to forget that old reliable, "peaceful." Since Gopac's publication, and in view of the Persian Gulf crisis, "warlike" might also fly. Consult your favorite focus group.

Half of you candidates, possibly, have received this neat list of suggestions, titled, "Language, a Key Mechanism of Control." It was sent to Republican candidates all over these United States.

Gopac is headed by Newt Gingrich, a partisan congressman who practices what he preaches.

•

Vote for Elvis

We citizens of these United States are led to understand—by the media, of course, that multi-dimensional mob referred to in the singular—that we're supposed to be pleased that a person who aspires to be president simply doesn't have a shot if he/she:

▸ Doesn't have congressional back-up;
▸ Can't get past various state protocols which restrict
ours to a two-party ochlocracy; and/or
▸ Just doesn't have enough time left before November
to achieve name recognition.

Little boys used to be told they could grow up to be president. For all I know—and hope—little girls are told they can, too, except perhaps in Utah. (And, naturally, the South.) My father told me, "Anybody can be president of these United States." He never once mentioned the above restrictions. He talked to me about hard work and ability and talents and beliefs. Inconsequential things like those. This was before charisma had been invented. Pop never once mentioned charisma.

No, I don't think my father actually believed his number-two son would become president. He had a pretty informed and suspicious view of politics. But I do think he believed it could actually happen, in the United States. In America. Without being backed up by a strong organization in Georgia or Oregon.

Would Pop have believed that we U.S. citizens have more of an opportunity, in 19-and-92, to vote unrestricted, free, in a triumph of our franchise and our freedoms, for an Elvis postage stamp than to vote for president?

You know, he probably would. He read history.

•

Keeping up Appearances

Nobody seems to have recorded whether Columbus hit the beaches looking regal. From his knees up, at any rate: it's probably tough to be regal with your cloak hems soaking wet. (On the other hand, General MacArthur eschewed a gangplank when he returned to the fray in World War II, and the wet-to-the-knees look worked for him.)

One can imagine a focus group of uncommitted natives scoping 'ol Chris out and trying to decide whether to welcome him and his gang, or kill them and divide their belongings at leisure. Presumably Columbus had some air about him—a few months at sea in a caravel was possibly sufficient—that carried the day. There is an unsubstantiated rumor that the vote was 51 percent for, 36 percent against. Fourteen percent went home to hide the women.

So much seems to hinge upon appearance, then as now. How many times have you heard in just the past few weeks that so-and-so "looks presidential." Looking presidential boils down to wearing a tailored suit, responding to light and/or sound, having some control over three facial expressions, and not picking your nose in public.

There really ought to be a little more to being president than that.

•

Horse racing

Just about every pundit, politico, columnist, egghead and talking head seems to agree with the proposition that presidential political campaigns should present carefully articulated, clearly detailed, insightful points of view and propose directions toward which the country should move. Most Americans concur.

Presidential campaigns, nearly everyone says, shouldn't be run as horse races are run. Naturally, that's the way they are conducted. Here comes Buchanan, coming up from Iowa to New Hampshire towards Arizona and South Carolina, thundering up the well-worn and muddy track, catching up to nose out Dole, who faded in the stretch. Alexander a possible third, but only lengths ahead of Forbes. Then comes Keyes and Lugar. Far behind is Dornan, clearly out-classed. Gramm was a scratch. And then there's Beedlebaum...in...the...rear.

Handicappers and odds-makers are clearly confused. Lots of early foot was shown, some staying power, a few good mudders, much fancy grooming, and quite a bit of jostling and interference. Foul claims galore. A few contestants headed completely in the wrong direction.

Yes, a funny way to choose the person to be president, the commander-in-chief, the one who can press the button and nuke us all back to the last extinction, the inspirational leader of the nation, most powerful person in the most powerful nation in the world.

Anybody laughing?

Notes From A Techno-Luddite

✎

Bugs

Some computer devices appear to be so easily corruptible it would take only a benign microbe to infect them. Some can be jimmied mechanically. So it made me pause when — in the recent presidential election — 55 percent of all votes cast were counted electronically by computers.

Programs used to run most of these computers are privately owned; localities and states simply purchase the programs and almost never adequately test them. Remember the talk about Lyndon Johnson in a cemetery copying names off gravestones? He reportedly remonstrated to a weary conspirator that, "All these other dead folks have a right to vote too, y'know."

Makes those times seem almost quaint.

Nowadays a computer jockey gives lectures on "safe computing," pointedly warning that, "When you share disks with someone, you've shared disks with everyone they've shared disks with."

Just say no.

•

No Sweat

"Land's End Direct Merchants" sells a lot of clothing-type stuff by catalog. None of it really fits me, so this is not a gratuitous column for which I might expect appropriate largesse to arrive by the unmarked truckload. (Besides, I don't have the knack of writing that genre. Darn.)

Land's End sells long underwear carrying the trademark

Thermaskin™ in which—to quote its November catalog, "the fibers have been permanently altered by something we call the Constant Comfort Process.

"Without too much scentific mumbo-jumbo (a phrase which should certainly help America in advancing literacy and beating out foreign competition for economic security in a technologic world), "let's just say that Thermaskin™ not only wicks sweat but attracts it for unrivaled evaporation."

Wow. But you ain't heard nothing yet. LE goes on: "H_2O (also known as sweat) is attracted to Thermaskin™ like ants to a picnic. Our Constant Comfort Process separates the 'H_2' from the 'O'...making evaporation take place much faster." Double zowee! How did they do that? There's even an accompanying stylized sketch showing the separation taking place.

Very impressive. Tell you what: If those cold fusion guys had only used sweat (also known as heavier water) in their laboratory jars, well, heck—they might still be holding press conferences.

P.S. If you find yourself in a closed room packed with people wicking sweat through altered polyester skins, better not light the fireplace. In certain concentrations "H_2" explodes.

•

Software Virus

My high-tech, sophisticated writing system has been struck down by a ballpoint pen ink-retentive virus: The dreaded Leonardo de Vinci strain. The worst.

Lately I've been having difficulty with my RAM, or random access memory. (I generally subscribe to the notion that it's not so much my internal circuitry wimping out: I just don't pay attention.) But I never thought my ballpoint pens—henceforth known as BPPs—would let me down. It took me decades to switch to BPPs from my trusty, but sometimes messy, fountain pen. Years of testing and grueling performance proofs. And now this!

I always store my BPPs in antiseptic circumstances and keep them under supervision. It's my practice to never, ever exchange ink cartridges on casual acquaintance with any baby boomer, nor to use my BPPs outside of drug-free zones. I do safe ballpoint.

Next thing you know the lines on yellow $8\frac{1}{2}$ x 11 paper tablets will start disappearing mysteriously. Then I'll be out of business.

No fair yelling, "Speed the Day."

•

Foolproof

This week a new camera and film system is to be introduced; it's supposed to be foolproof.

Well, no one tried it out on this fool. The wholly new system—developed by a consortium of Canon, Fuji, Kodak, Minolta and Nikon—includes a new film contained within a self-loading cartridge. The cartridge contains bar code and magnetic data recording used in processing. Pictures can be shot in three formats. And there aren't going to be any "bugs."

I have trouble with "push here, dummy" cameras—and here come new ones, with new film that costs 20 percent more. I think I'll wait until this new camera system can fax directly to my non-existent fax machine, or e-mail to friends all over the place—who of course don't have computers. Either. That should get me to the next foolproof era.

Energy

I ran across a statistic that darn near turned my brain's remaining circuitry to "On." *Science News* reports that computers collectively consume an estimated five percent of U.S. commercial electric energy production. Even more startling—to me, anyhow—it is believed that most of the time the United States 30 to 35 million personal computers are turned on, but not being used.

What a waste of energy. Greenhouse-ing to no purpose and all that. Ah, but think of the worst damage to the planet and its inhabitants should the doggone things be in use all that time...

Hello? Hello?
Anybody there?

Just me, Mouse.

De-Copy This

The Ricoh Company is a Japanese producer of office equipment. It also makes cameras, video things, and who knows what else. Ricoh recently announced it has developed a machine that erases photocopies. Put copies in one end and out zips a blank piece of paper at the other.

The mind boggles. To put matters in perspective, I still believe personal computers, rock-and-roll, and any audio system since vinyl 33 1/3 records are passing fads.

The first photocopier outfits never promised their machines would save paper, although computer companies certainly did. The promised "paperless office" hasn't materialized; offices are now overwhelmed with paper, whose use has skyrocketed. One office-equipment observer suggests this new device may be an industry attempt "to assuage some of its ecological guilt."

Ricoh plays on the recycling angle, stating it's cheaper to recycle copier paper with its new system than it is to recycle by conventional methods — and it can be accomplished right in your own office! Whee. No more trips to the recycling center.

I shall forego the obvious and not indicate how society would be advanced should Ricoh and its fellow culprits simply build a machine that makes photocopies, laser prints and faxes — and sends them directly through the erasing process.

•

The Opiate of the Masses

Two of the columns that appear in the *Jackson Hole News* are written by Paul Bruun. Both appear under his name. That should tell you a lot.

There are no secrets safe from Paul Bruun. And apparently no way for him to keep one. Why, decades ago he told me and everyone in the vicinity that I don't bend zee knees when I ski...a tiny fault he detected from a full quarter-mile away. From a speeding car going in the opposite direction. That should tell you more.

Now he goes ahead and discloses that not only do I not use a word processor, but also that everything I write is by hand.

Horrors. If Paul only knew all the rest: I don't have a CB (remember them?), nor a CD. No stereo. No cellulite phone. No scanner, no fax machine, no beeper. I am a dinosaur, and old fossils simply have fewer necessity-needs than do Yuppies. Like Paul.

I have, in fact, tried to go from pen-and-ink to the typewriter, but I went to school prior to the Machine Age. Barely avoided clay tablets. I don't type. Paul may possibly not know that and surely doesn't give a busted fish line—but he started this.

Paul, I tried to learn. I have failed to learn in probably eight adult typing classes. I even took a personal computer class for adults. There were no computers, actually, in the classroom. We did troop down to a showroom where we could look at one. I left unenlightened.

My advice, Paul, is not to mistake form for substance in your future letter-perfect, spell-checked, fully "justified" writings.

Quoth the dinosaur: The personal computer is now become the opiate of the masses. (All rights reserved.)

•

Fun in Cyberspace

My friends, whom I respect for their superior intelligence and knowledge, tell me—and tell me—how wonderful it is to have a personal computer. I am almost ready to concede that a human being is without worth unless he is computer literate, up-to-date, and linked to cyberspace.

A few of my prospective mentors even suggest it's fun to compute. They might even be right. Take the following authentic-appearing AP news story that appeared recently on a computer bulletin board — whatever *that* is — on the internet:

"Microsoft Bids to Acquire Catholic Church"

> Vatican City (AP) — In a joint press conference in St. Peter's Square this morning, Microsoft Corp. and the Vatican announced that the Redmond, Ore., software giant will acquire the Roman Catholic Church in exchange for "an unspecified number of shares of Microsoft common stock." With the acquisition, Pope John Paul II will become the senior vice president of the combined company's new Religious Software Division, while Microsoft senior vice presidents Michael Maples and Steven Ballmer will be invested in the College of Cardinals, said Microsoft chairman Bill Gates.

It was, of course, a joke. A pretty good one. Went on to provide details of the deal, including Microsoft's plans to license electronic rights to the Bible. To offer sacraments on-line. Like that.

Rush Limbo is said to have read this bogus press release on his TV program and, in response, some of his humorless listeners complained to Microsoft. Soon, the real AP and the (real) Microsoft Corp. issued denials, clarifications and apologies to "anyone who was offended by the (electronic) document." Humor is as humor does.

To his great credit, a spokesman for the Roman Catholic Church in western Oregon both understood the obvious prank and responded with jovial enthusiasm. "Offended?" he asked. "We thought our prayers had finally been answered!"

He issued an (official) news release of his own, headlined, "Church Hopes Dashed As Microsoft Denies Acquisition Bill." Listed were a number of reasons why a church/Microsoft deal might have been mutually beneficial:

▸ "We've had 2,000 years of working with icons.
Microsoft has only done it for three. We could have helped."

▸ "We could have introduced Father-On-Line. No wait,
no hours, no congestion in the church parking lot."

Fun in cyberspace. Who would have guessed?

•

Toilets and Bulldozers

Sometimes I wonder which of two constants in developed countries has contributed most to environmental degradation and man's basic unawareness of his place in the natural world: the flush toilet or earthmoving equipment. Both are indelible examples of the Law of Unexpected Results, a close cousin to ol' Murphy's Law.

First, Thomas Crapper's contribution to mankind. Crapper (his real name) invented the flush toilet in the 1800s. Then, as now, safe drinking water was of fundamental concern to man. Primarily because of health issues, long before Crapper's invention early man learned not to eliminate in his source of drinking water, and to drink upstream of where his animals live and die. Then too, nature provided bacterial agents that disposed of urine and fecal matter. Given sufficient time and a relatively small amount of organic material to contend with, natural systems worked.

Nomadic man probably avoided most sanitary problems — or at least he could *see* them. A pile of dung or a pool of stinking water was easily discernable. Not pleasant, but one knew just where it was.

What is called progress in mankind's dealing with such matters evolved as man began to overpopulate the earth. A system of sewers and running sluices were developed in towns and cities. Some higher civilizations even learned to use excrement to fertilize their crops, accommodating the bacteria, viruses and who-knows-what-all that was recycled into their food. Then came the flush toilet. Out of sight. Out of mind. Waste happens, but you don't have to *do* anything about it but flush. So nobody really cares. It's out of the house, out of town, downstream of your water source. Of course, *you* are downstream of somebody else's waste…

Sewage treatment plants based on natural processes were created by discerning physicians and their allies, and have been keeping developed countries slightly ahead of catastrophic disease since the late 19th century. If politicians and civil engineers were not in command of these plants, by default, I'd be a bit more confident that mankind's obsession with overpopulating the planet won't soon overwhelm the stolid mini-advances made in sewage treatment procedures.

In large part I blame Crapper's flush toilet. If each of us had to consider each day the consequences of our living on earth, attitudes towards sanitary practices, procreation, urbanization and wanton destruction of the environment — little things like that — would change. We don't have to, so we won't.

Consider now the bulldozer and its allies. Earth moving equipment has made it cheaper to level anything, including mountains, in order to build…things. To rip up forests just to have a space to move the darn yellow machines of destruction around. Remember when farmers used to contour till? Shucks. Now fields are made laser-flat, contours eliminated along with any wildlife that once took refuge in the fringes. Huge machines daily rip away incomprehensible tonnage of cleverly labeled "overburden" or "spoil" to get at the treasures of our exhaustible planet.

Bulldozers remove the necessity of considering drainage, natural hazards, or future concerns of any kind at all. Flatten, rip down, level and build. Take the profit and run.

You may not agree with my choices of the worst technological advances. Perhaps you'd choose waste of resources, ocean overfishing, the loss of civility in society, lousy public education. or the mountain bike.

Choose your own villains.

•

Voice Mail

Once upon a time (always a catchy start), dinosaurs used rotary phones to reach someone they wished to speak to. The intended party was reached — or not. There were no interceding answering machines. If the party was reached, acceptance or rejection of the matter at hand proceeded.

Ah, but now comes the automated phone system, a computerized elevator voice that purrs directions, a menu, and instructions to press a series of buttons ad nauseum. If you don't get cut-off, you eventually reach "voice mail." Silly me, I expect by this time in my quest I can speak, have my message recorded and, sometime or other, be heard by my intended listener. And, praise be, responded to.

As far as I know, this cycle of events has been satisfactorily completed twice in the past decade. Okay, I'm exaggerating. Once.

Foreign Competition
✎

We showed 'em

Two 20th century technological achievements which I consider have had the deepest impact upon human behavior — deep down gut influences — are the personal computer and wind chill factor. Even though each of these triumphs has made life miserable for the typing illiterate and anybody who simply wants to know the outside temperature, they are certainly milestones in the evolution of what we carelessly call sophistication. No argument.

But now — as the century approaches its end — comes an even more innovative, startling, and remarkable evolutionary leap: the portable, collapsible, courtside changing booth. A female tennis player can now change her shirt during match breaks.

And here we are, trying to improve our schools and our entire approach to education because we're supposed to be technologically behind the Japanese.

Hah! We showed 'em.

•

Way to go

The speaker of the lower house of Japan's parliament, one Mr. Sakurauchi, declared last month that American workers are lazy and that one-third of them can't read. Friends who are gainfully employed assure me that the bit about American workers being lazy is not entirely correct.

Sakurauchi's partially wrong about the literacy matter, too: Only six percent of our working age population is totally illiterate. But — and its a big but — fewer than half of Americans between 21 and 25 are said by the U.S. Department of Education to possess the level of literacy skill required to succeed in today's world.

A worker from a Detroit assembly plant, mad as hell at Sakurauchi's statement, held up a hand-lettered sign of protest, photographed and widely distributed, which read: "Japan said your (sic) lazy No to Japanese imports."

What *was* Sakaruachi thinking?

•

Caveat Emptor

China has just passed a law, to take effect this September, making the production and sale of shoddy goods a crime. Penalties range from seven years in prison to execution.

Gee whiz. It's going to be tough to integrate China into the world economy that way: This simply isn't the consumerism ethic developed countries are accustomed to. What has happened to caveat emptor, the great principle that keeps American consumers flocking to the stores? Somehow.

More or less on this topic, I now and again ponder what Mr. Iacocca, late of Chrysler Corporation, meant by his now frequently copied statement: "When you're in the automobile business, you've got to lead, follow, or get out of the way."

What the devil does that mean? What does it say? What should the penalty be for sales pitches like this?

If China penalizes shoddy manufacturing and also demands truth in advertising, we'd better make friends.

Or, as the saying goes, get out of the way.

Early Man

Meg's Theory of Evolution

The axe found with the mummified body of a man discovered on the Similuan Glacier of Austria in September 1991, has been determined to be nearly pure copper and not bronze (which is copper alloyed with tin). This determination—plus a couple of radio-carbon dates on pieces of woven mat this chap was carrying—has pushed his estimated time of death back to at least 4,600 years ago. He is, thus, a pre-Bronze Age man from the late Neolithic period.

Remarkable. We are talking about a real old-timer here, folks. Austria and Italy are squabbling over in which present-day country he was actually found, so snippets of the mummy itself haven't yet been dated; last things first, as usual. In any case, this ol' boy is at least as old as you feel some mornings.

Okay, as old as I feel.

In addition to his wood-shafted axe, he was toting a little leather pouch with flint and kindling, a flint knife, a wood-reinforced leather quiver with 14 feather-tipped arrows, plus an emergency quick-fix kit composed of replacement arrowheads and a kind of putty which may be made from pitch. A sophisticated person.

His clothes were mostly leather and fur, lined with grasses or hay. He wore a stone necklace and a birch bark fanny pack—not to forget tattoos on the inside of his knee and on his back above his kidneys. All in all, the kind of fellow you might meet on your next glacier climb, or at your favorite eatery.

A non-related finding last year concluded that Neanderthal man lived in Western Europe as recently as 36,000 years ago. Thus, Neanderthals were hanging around several thousand years after the first modern humans appeared in that area.

It is generally accepted that modern humans descended from Cro-Magnons, and Neanderthals slowly disappeared. I say "generally accepted" not only because some scientists reject the co-existence finding but because — far more importantly — the Muse doesn't. She is working on an original thesis that proves more than one species of modern man co-exists today. Her learned dissertation aside, she invites you simply to look around.

•

Fire

A while back early hominids, no doubt after watching or running away from a fire, figured out how to use it for their own purposes, thus foregoing the presumed delights of sushi and wild game tartare until later. Much later, it turns out.

New archeologic evidence from South Africa indicates the discovery of fire occurred there at least one million years ago, possibly as long ago as 1.5 million years. Only a decade ago the earliest persuasive evidence of fire used deliberately went back only 500,000 years, in present-day China.

Pretty exciting stuff. In discussing topics such as this, archeologists and guys in related fields tend to get really expansive. "Intentional use of fire is the most momentous event in human prehistory." Or, "Everything we take for granted is connected to the technology of fire." Well, it's that or tool making, or agriculture, or astronomical comprehension, or whatever else was the particular authority's master thesis. Perhaps it's more significant that in Africa fossil evidence of two human ancestors was found with the remnants of the first barbeque: Homo erectus — a direct ancestor — and Australopithecus robustus, a big-ape man line that died out a million years ago.

I wonder how ol' Australopithecus would react if he found out that a million years later those erectus types were still huddled together wondering just what to do with this fire thing.

•

Neanderthal Barbie

For those who appreciate a bit of whimsy — and for whoever recalls when an artifact found on the National Elk Refuge aroused fanciful speculation — below is a letter the Paleoanthropology Division of the Smithsonian Institution sent a man who routinely sent it items he believed to be of enormous scientific value. The *Journal of Irreproducible Results* edited the Smithsonian's response, but hoped its essence wasn't changed.

I don't think it was.

• • •

Dear Sir,

Thank you for your latest submission to the Institution, labeled "Hominid Skull." We have given this specimen a careful and detailed examination, and regret to inform you that we disagree with your theory that it represents conclusive proof of the presence of Early Man two million years ago. Rather, it appears that what you have found is the head of a Barbie doll, of the variety of Malibu Barbie™.

There are a number of physical attributes of the specimen which might have tipped you off to its modern origin: The material is molded plastic; ancient hominid remains are typically frozen fossilized bone. The cranial capacity is approximately nine cubic centimeters, well below the threshold of even the earliest identified proto-hominids. The dentition pattern is more consistent with the common domesticated dog that it is with "ravenous man-eating Pliocene clams" you speculate roamed the wet-lands during that time.

Without going into too much detail, let us say that: A: The specimen looks like the head of a Barbie doll that a dog has chewed on. B: Clams don't have teeth.

"I got fire. Wanna go on a date?"

Space

Voyager 2

At first I thought it was Ol' Doc's chart on me: "Groping in the dim vastness far from home, arthritic and partly deaf, feeble of voice and prone to memory lapses..."

But no, it was the lead on an article by John N. Wilford about Voyager 2. What a great old Tiger! Despite symptoms Wilford identified as a "failed radio receiver, computer glitches, creaky instrument platform and other manifestations of advancing age," Voyager keeps on keeping on, showing everyone how astonishingly different each planetary world is from every other one.

Early on its Grand Tour, Voyager took unforgettable pictures of our little planet, blue and brown and white against the void. Just by looking at the photograph intelligent life on Earth cannot be detected, and upon closer examination...

But I digress. All hail! Voyager 2. Keep on keeping on, old timer.

•

Hubble Trouble

I had discarded the notion of commenting upon the Hubble Space Telescope's troubles. I had really hoped the instrument would work and, anyhow, just about every writer, comic and barfly has taken a shot at it. Besides, if you've ever been a participant when some new gadget or system gets turned on for the first time, you know that if it's successful it has a hundred fathers. If not...

Heck, I've got a vehicle that keeps me on edge every time I turn its ignition key.

I'm breaking my silence because I simply don't have faith in the Hubble investigation panel, in good part because Richard Feynmann has died. Dr. Feynmann was the guy who dunked a hunk of the gasket materials used in the space shuttle boosters into a glass of ice water; when he flexed the stuff, it broke—a little demonstration that moved the panel investigating space shuttle Challenger's explosion right along.

The Hubble was not tested as a system. It could have been tested. It should have been tested. It wasn't. Now it turns out there were two mirrors built for the Hubble. One of them is stored in a crate on Earth; it wasn't tested either. It was a back-up mirror, not a bad idea. Some skeptics think it was ground better than the one in space. But—the guessing goes—Perkin-Elmer, the prime contractor, simply didn't want to use equipment built by a competitor, Kodak.

Pride, you know. It goeth...nowhere sometimes.

•

Apollo Memories

Twenty-five years ago man first walked on the moon. It was a substantial technological achievement, as gutsy a venture as they come, and an example of human curiosity and humanity itself. As it worked out, Americans went to the moon first, and so far only Americans have been there.

Twenty-five years ago. Back in a time of our country's history when wallets were certainly no fatter than they are now, Americans chose to look at problems and opportunities and say, "We can do that." Now we mostly recite, mindlessly and numbingly, "We can't afford it."

That was back in a time when our belief was that our nation's people working in concert with government could accomplish good and even great things. A time before the notion was perniciously spread — and accepted — that government is, and must be, some absolute evil.

The Apollo moon landings of a quarter century ago were thrilling, were great achievements, great voyages. They certainly thrilled Meg and me. We resented reporter Walter Cronkite's having become bored with them and his doing so much to influence the public in turn to become bored — yet basking in the celebrity of Mr. Space Commentator.

Ah. I see I still resent it.

Once I touched a piece of the moon. Shucks, I was one of probably 2,000 people who touched the rock on that day, that week. Probably millions have touched that moon piece by now. But I went through the line four times.

I still remember the way it felt.

•

Meteorites

A meteorite found in Antarctica in 1984 is thought to contain evidence of primitive life on Mars that existed some 3.6 billion years ago.

The meteorite in question is known as ALH84001, which identifies it as the first meteorite found during the 1984 United States National Science Foundation meteorite-searching season, and that it was found in the Allan hills region of Antarctica.

Meteorite-searching in Antarctica is productive because these space objects, which have made it through Earth's atmosphere, often remain upon the surface of that continent; they don't get covered by soil affected by biological activity. In the 13,000 years ALH84001 had lain on the surface of that polar continent, it was exposed to fewer airborne contaminants than it would have been on most other land forms.

Antarctica is, for many reasons, a splendid, unique scientific resource for our world. The United States has had research bases there since 1928, and a dominant national presence there since the 1950s.

Who can tell what other meteorites can be discovered, what hints concerning future global temperatures, what insights into life on Earth remain to be found?

So what are we, the recently enlightened peoples of these United States about to do? We are considering giving up our presence, our base, at the South Pole. What the heck: it's only having the US. remain a player in setting policy for the entire continent (as in striving to keep the region free of military endeavors).

Besides, we could buy five C-130 cargo planes with the budget for our South Pole activities. Moreover, we could be spared those discouraging reports about ozone holes, those silly predictions of global climate change, and all those research papers with those hilarious titles certain lawmakers and talk show jockeys like to poke fun at.

My. What a deal.

The Yellowstone Fires

✎

Put It Out

Although my knowledge of the subject is limited—and some of it old—I understand the arguments supporting the beneficial results of forest and range fires.

I know that nutrients are released and go back into the soil and are used; that habitats are altered and often ultimately improved; that some plant species including evergreens have evolved to require fire to reproduce; that openings in forests bring animal diversification and improved browse; that some believe various plant infestations or diseases are sometimes controlled. All that good stuff.

I recognize that if carbon and hydrogen didn't react with oxygen, this wouldn't be a blue planet, the only one yet known with life and rudimentary intelligence. And yet...

Yet when a forest fire starts in July in the third and worst year of drought and the potential for it to become exceedingly large—because of the dry conditions or the available fuel or persistent weather patterns—then not only guidelines and policies should be considered, but also the circumstances. Guidelines are just that, and should be altered when the situation demands it. If they cannot, why have people at all?

Policies can be altered, modified or set aside, if necessary. Even in a let-it-burn zone, a fire can be extinguished if the danger exceeds the benefits.

I know that the policies on fires in national parks, forests and wildernesses were set with great care and after a lot of consideration. But I'd bet not with prolonged drought of this unexpected nature, persistence and extent in mind.

Herewith, then, a Raynes rule: When in drought, put it out.

•

From the gut

The counterman/waiter/probable part owner of a cafe in West Yellowstone—a comfortable, ill-lit, poorly laid-out, one step above a greasy spoon, where the talk is often better than the cafe grub—was talking to two guys from Virginia sporting funny hats.

"Oh, those acreages they give about the fires in the parks are based on the total area within the fire perimeters; but within those perimeters only fifty percent of the area in actually burned. There are unburned trees and places."

Then, after a moment of reflection, he blurted out, "But my little daughter will never see Yellowstone the way I did. She never will. Why, the whole Firehole Canyon is gone, black on both sides!"

We were sitting there openly listening, drinking coffee, and reading a day-old Fire Line Update in the Greater Yellowstone Command in which this citizen's first remark could be found, almost word for word. We hope and expect that 50 percent estimate is pretty close. Unburned areas, surviving trees, patches of green and life itself remain after a forest fire is out.

On the other hand, total acreages involved are the only statistics given on all those informational signs in national forests everywhere. We don't recall ever seeing signs with headings or caveats indicating that "these acreages should really be divided by half because a mosaic of burned and unburned forests and meadows remains when forest fires ultimately are extinguished."

As for his second comment? That one came from his gut. Nobody reading this column—or writing it—who saw Yellowstone National Park before July 1988 will see Yellowstone the way it was. Ever.

•

Smokey Bear

Last fall I believed that, after 43 years, Smokey Bear had come to the end of his professional usefulness. In a moment of mourning I created a painting as an epitaph to Smokey and gave it to Bridger-Teton National Forest spokesman Fred Kingwill, thinking he might perhaps use it for some nefarious purpose or other.

Now, however, good ol' Smoke has been brought back. He's wiser. Lots wiser. He now says that only fires caused by man's carelessness are bad. Land managers (Smokey's handlers) have made a complete conversion. For a 100-plus years, European and American forestry experts held that "forestry would not be possible if surface fires were tolerated." This is according to S.J. Pyne of Arizona State University. In 1989 foresters now say with equal conviction, according to Pyne, that "forestry and land management would be impossible if prescribed surface fires were excluded."

Welcome back, Smoke, but be wary. Next they're gonna put you on a diet, slim you down, make you exercise and learn computers. A small caveat, Old Bear, courtesy of John Sloan: "It may be taken as an axiom that the majority is always wrong on cultural matters."

"Look, Monica—It's Smokey Bear!"

A Bargain

When I read that, thus far, fighting the Yellowstone fires has cost $106 million, I was impressed by the sum. But then I almost simultaneously read that a single song-and-dance guy has raked in $97 million in 1987 alone.

It made the firefighting seem like a damn bargain. To my knowledge, I've never heard or seen Michael Jackson except on a TV commercial. I mean not to express judgment upon his work — or the lasting worth of his talents — when I confess the Greater Yellowstone Ecosystem is worth more.

•

Huh?

I read in the paper that "the fires may destroy certain life forms — some insects, reptiles and nesting birds — but they are not greatly affected."

Well, *this* life form would feel greatly affected if destroyed by fire.

•

A Time to Mourn

"Look," said the managing editor, "have you written your column yet?"

I looked. "Nope, but it will be another perceptive, insightful and memorable..."

"Because, " he continued, "we're doing an edition on the fires ("the fires" are the 1988 Yellowstone ecosystem fires, of course) and we'd like you to write about them this week."

"Why? You know I have a somewhat different overall view about them and their legacy than the standard line and..."

"Yes," the editor allowed. "And we'd appreciate your off-beat approach, so..."

"Well." (I was taking this all as flattery.) "Sure. On your head. Since you said 'please.' Glad to. Why not."

Wait a moment. Isn't there a major fire exhibit at Grant Village in Yellowstone featuring our exalted editor and publisher, and what he believes about the fires? Yes, his letter to his daughter, Alexis. Careful 'ol buddy: This could be a set-up. Aw, what the heck; he has integrity.

Besides, I agree with him. A new biological succession will occur in Yellowstone. (Although I might add that that assumes no greenhouse effect, or another immediate Ice Age, acid rain, or some other unforeseen ugliness around the corner.) I agree with Superintendent Barbee when he writes that there is a new attraction, a memorable lesson in wilderness processes, and a chance to witness—if you're Alexis' age—wilderness regeneration on a scale rarely seen on earth.

It is exciting. It can be informative, and I hope what is learned is made available to the public as soon as it becomes known. I have lived long enough to have seen burned forests regrow. I won't see Yellowstone accomplish it, and I'm beginning to accept the Grand Teton Beaver Creek burn is the way that area will look in my time.

The thing is, I feel that even as the Yellowstone region fires were raging uncontrolled and uncontrollable last year, even as no one could even guess what might happen next or where, the American public was shoved and spin-doctored right past decent grieving—let alone the possibility that perhaps too many thousands of acres were burning up. Let alone that birds and other animals were perishing.

We were hustled into admiring anticipation of the new season, the reawakening of life to come, without even a backward glance at the corpse. Whisked past any consideration of possible failure of park and forest policies and administration directly into expectation of the wonders of nature, and how a new cycle of future forest had begun.

We were never given a chance to mourn.

It's hard to believe park operators don't comprehend that people — the people who own the parks — take home memories of them. Here, right *here*, we saw that unforgettable sunset, and *there* we watched the bear and her two cubs. And *yonder's* where we camped and it rained and blew so hard it flattened the tent.

Favorite spots, treasured recollections. If they are gone, we miss them. I would have liked to have a chance to say farewell. Did you ever go to a funeral service in which the deceased doesn't even seem to be mentioned? Contrast that with the service in which the departed's life is extolled and the pleasure he brought to his family and friends is warmly recollected. Each one will ask for faith in the future, but which one leaves family and friends comforted?

Information managers during and since the fires of 1988 often deride press coverage which, they say, gave a misimpression that the whole darn ecosystem is in ashes. They release pictures of elk or bison calmly grazing as fire rages immediately beyond.

Certainly. It has been pointed out — Faith McNulty, a fine nature writer comes to mind — that even in emergencies animals do what they are programmed to do. Grazing animals graze. Predators respond to a sudden availability of prey. Burrowing animals go underground. Birds fly. Fish swim.

And much of the park burned. Bureaucratic agencies, governmental or corporate, dissemble, evade and resist stating facts.

I know that fire is an integral part of the ecology and that plants and animals are adapted and have evolved to survive as species, some to thrive. I know that if correct studies are made and conducted over the long-term, a wonderful opportunity to see a large burned area in the Rockies has become available.

I know that the thermal regions, the large vistas, the glorious ecosystem yet remain. I know periodic large fires are typical for this region. I know that nearly all of the plant communities in Greater Yellowstone look the way they do precisely because of recurrent fires in the past.

Trouble is, I also know that the pre-1988 burn, computerized policy in Yellowstone was based — at least in part — on the notion that Yellowstone was comparatively nonflammable.

In light of all this history of fire now paraded for us to acknowledge, that do beat all.

And so I have what I feel is an understandably cautious attitude about the flood of glad tidings pouring out about rebirth, re-awakening, nature at her good works. Take that last phrase back: Nature does know what's she's all about. We have yet adequately to understand her.

My post-fire survey has been limited to the roads, short excursions, and one flight over the southern one-sixth of the park and surrounding ecosystem. I have only impressions. It seems to me that mostly it was conifers that burned, not aspens or willows. Riparian areas seem relatively untouched. New growth varies from none in heavily burned areas to lush in meadows and at the edges of burns.

I see lots of accumulated fuel — dead and living material which can and will burn — in unburned areas. Should we torch the rest of the area? Should we have hoped for more acreage to have burned last year to get it over with for a few hundred years? Is jumping in with both feet on every ignition of any origin this year simply political (I bet) and not based upon knowledge gained in '88 (you bet)?

I carp about this as much as the public relations guys rant. Dammit, the greater Yellowstone ecosystem *is* precious — to everyone who has seen it or will, even to those who can never experience its special wonders. Yellowstone is the world's first national park, an unequivocally good idea that originated here and was exported around the globe.

A person's accumulated fuel load of passion occasionally flares up about what goes on in his parks.

The Environment

Slick Operators

My readers no doubt expect a reasoned and thoughtful perspective on the Exxon Valdez oil spill. We are, after all, a civilized society in which risks and benefits are carefully considered, each given equal weight, before actions are taken.

There are, after all, rules and regulations, environmental protection laws, a growing awareness that we live on a tiny planet protected only by a thin and vulnerable shield of mutable gases. We have many organizations which respond to what we are all assured is a worldwide ground swell of environmental concern and which keep up on problems old and new. After all, we are the reasoning animal able to use foresight, let alone hindsight.

You bet.

Yet, after all, one cannot help yielding to overwhelming urges to flail about — helplessly, uselessly, without a sense of relief — at each bulletin from Prince William Sound. At every interview of some politician or bureaucrat or corporate mouthpiece. At every prediction of damages done. At oil-covered square mileage the area of this state or that country. At the pat-them-on-the head solemn pronouncements that we can drill for oil in the Arctic National Wildlife Refuge with environmental responsibility...and should the impossible ever happen, we know how to prevent any real damage. Unless we don't. However, we simply have to take risks, because this is not a risk-free world.

What bull. What predictable, interminable, dreary, sticks-to-the-barn-wall, bull. What it boils down to is man is blindly determined do whatever he wants to do, to whatever or whomever he wants to do it to, with anything he chooses to do it with.

And he'll all the while be as unctuous and sanctimonious and blandly reassuring to the unthinking and powerless masses as he needs or cares to be. If Earth really becomes uninhabitable, why man will simply move out into space.

But before we get to go to that condo on the prime dark side of the moon, we have to endure a record-setting, spin-doctoring spectacle at Valdez. Forget the 11 million gallons of ever-spreading crude oil. Ignore all those dying fish and birds and animals and organisms up and down the chain of life. Let's just get Exxon Captain Joseph Hazelwood hanging from the yardarm; that'll make it all right. Throw the masses a scapegoat for this despoiled coastal waterway. That oughta satisfy them.

Then let's run back up to the coastal plain in the Arctic National Wildlife Refuge and do it again.

Arrogance

Are you familiar with clingage? (No, not cleavage. Clingage.) That's the industry name for residue left inside an emptied oil tanker's tanks. It's a waxy substance that is difficult to scrape off. So, when Exxon Valdez was cleaned for its tow from Alaskan waters to San Diego for repair, clingage remained.

California waters are 30 degrees warmer than Alaskan waters. You can guess what happened. You can, but Exxon couldn't and the U.S. Coast Guard didn't.

"We knew the tanks had not been cleaned thoroughly on the way down, but no one foresaw that the warmer climate would change (the nature of clingage)," said the Coast Guard spokesperson.

The arrogance and complacency remain unchecked.

•

Global Warming

Our little planet has warmed and cooled constantly over time. It's just getting out of its last ice age, and that was only this morning, as epochs go. No real debate there.

The "global warming" of present interest centers around whether industrial, automotive and other by-products of human activity have created a heat-trapping "greenhouse," what that means to life on Earth, and if the process is reversible.

The threat of global warming is a persuasive hypothesis. Its proof requires such a time scale—decades or half centuries—that it can be argued there's no evidence yet of a problem. Don't worry; stay cool.

The troubling thing is that the no-worry guys are the same clear-thinkers who pooh-poohed evidence of the atmosphere's thinning ozone layer a little less than 20 years ago, and lost for us all a dozen years of serious attempts to curtail specific chemical contamination.

Because these particular chaps are now saying global warming is a myth does not, by itself, offer any substantial verification we have already entered uncontrolled warming, but it is exceedingly difficult to give their opinions objective consideration.

To me, one of the corollaries to the global warming hypothesis, little mentioned, is perhaps the scariest: On the way to an overall temperature rise of three, four or nine degrees Fahrenheit, there will be increasingly severe weather events and cycles. Temperature extremes. Hurricanes of extraordinary strength. More tornadoes and cyclones. Severe droughts and floods.

Every one of my dwindling number of correspondents interested in the natural world has mentioned unusual weather wherever he is on the continent. They mention that weather records — short term as they are — are being smashed, and note changes in bird and animal occurrences and populations.

Really now: Can I, should I, stack up my particular weirdo pals and their field notes, as well as mine, against expressions by appointees with transient political agendas? Should you?

You bet. The odds are good, darn it.

•

The Deregulators

The Quayle Quarterly, a mildly irreverent publication which a couple of my more enlightened friends take, is devoted to the matter of Vice President Quayle. It pokes fun at Quayle by providing his actual statements, managing to be amusing and scary simultaneously, somewhat of a tour de force.

The Quarterly must be wrestling with a major problem nowadays. It seems J. Danforth has become active—albeit behind the scenes—and has found a cause. He is becoming a leading administration environmental deregulator. Which suggests to me that he ought to keep looking for honest work.

Mr. Quayle heads up something called The White House Council on Competitiveness. (Don't you sometimes marvel at some of these names?) Other members are Mr. Darman, director of the Office of Management and Budget; Mr. Brady, secretary of treasury; Mr. Mossbacker, secretary of commerce; Mr. Boskin, chairman of the Council of Economic Advisers; Attorney General Mr. Barr; and Mr. Sununu, White House chief of staff. Does it come as a surprise that this line-up (stacked, one might say) is beholden exclusively to business interests? Not hardly.

Congress is investigating the role of this outfit in seeking relief from—rather than firmly enforcing—environmental regulations. The council has become the major behind-the-scenes player in revising the Wetlands Delineation Manual to lose half of the paltry remaining marshy acres; in messing with the 1990 Clean Air Law so that it will, among other offenses, allow some 34,000 pollution sources to increase the amount of pollution they generate merely by notifying their respective states they plan to do so; in declaring it has oversight of virtually every scrap of paper issued by any federal agency, regardless of the laws enacted by Congress.

All done in secret. Even Congress has been unable to get free access to files denoting the Council's role in making regulatory policy. The White House—whoever he or she is—told the Council simply not to let Congress know what it was doing to its laws and the function of government agencies. Congress suspects, reasonably, that it is being bypassed. To me, this is all summed up in a recent *New Yorker* cartoon by Bernard Schoenbaum, in which one overbearing three-button-suit-type declaims to a stunned listener, "I may not know much about the Constitution, but I certainly know what I like."

Merciful heavens. That might be the Council's motto.

•

Ozone

Stratospheric, protective ozone is being depleted at near-record rates. It's about 15 percent lower than levels recorded at the same time in the past five years; 1992 is predicted to be the fourth straight year for record stratospheric ozone depletion.

Simultaneously, atmospheric pollutant ozone concentrations have recently been discovered by satellites over Brazil and southern Africa. These unexpectedly large concentrations are believed to be the result of massive biomass burning on those two continents; one hypothesis postulates the fire emissions are comparable to those from fossil-fuel combustion in northern latitudes. Nobody is predicting, yet, whether these newly established ozone concentrations are leading to net warming or to net cooling of the earth.

It might be instructive to reflect how presumably intelligent life can investigate — scientifically and carefully — the effects and causation of atmospheric conditions on Venus and Mars, yet let politicians and sycophants describe what is happening to Earth's support system.

Nah.

Just party down.

For the Birds

Raven or Crow

Jack Huyler passed on this field identification tip when trying to decide if you're looking at a crow or raven. Crows have 10 flight, or pinion, feathers. Ravens, Jack says, have 11 pinions. So...it's just a matter of a pinion.

•

Field-guide-itis

Field guides tend to emphasize males in breeding plumage and not birds in some transitional phase or in winter; often, female birds are slighted. (Hmm. I should write a field guide to female and juvenile birds. Down with sexism.)

I think it was Ogden Nash who wrote:

I wonder why the
Birdies never look
Like the birdies
In the birdie book?

I say I think Ogden Nash wrote that, because I've gone through four of his compilations without finding that verse. Maybe it wasn't Nash. Perhaps it was Donald Trump.

Lacking Trump's flair for memorable, poetic quotations and his understanding of justice, I always remind birdwatchers of the poor, unfortunate people who don't exhibit their own incredible physiques or statuesque voluptuousness, respectively. Think of a *Guide to Birdwatchers*, where every male is described as 6'2', 185 pounds, armspread of 74", clean-shaven, and every female is 5'7", 128 pounds, 38/23/34.

In real life, sad to say, some birdwatchers look like me. Or you. Same with birds.

•

Hummin' Home

In three otherwise unrelated conversations this week the subject of bird migration came up — in particular, hummingbird migration. In all three it was suggested that hummingbirds "piggyback" their way south under the wings of Canada geese.

Bird migration has long fascinated people. There are references to it in the Bible, and by writers dating back to Aristotle. He thought certain bird species hibernate, passing the winter in hollow trees or in mud marshes. Swallows, storks, kites and doves were included in his hibernation theory, which persisted for two millenia.

Current migration theories are based on methods not available in Aritstotle's time, including bird banding, radar observations, and better communication among birdwatchers. We have more information and fewer myths; nevertheless, there are still unknowns and unsolved mysteries.

Hummingbird migration isn't one of them. Western hummers such as the Calliope, Rufous and Broad-tailed use overland migration routes, precluding the need for hitch-hiking knowhow. The Ruby-Throated Hummingbird, found east of the 100th meridian, crosses the Gulf of Mexico — more than 500 miles of open sea — in a single sustained flight. Twice a year.

If one thinks of those little wings beating up to 100 times a second for a full day of unrelieved flying it's...well, it's almost unbelievable. No wonder the idea of piggy-backing is attractive. Not all that long ago, *Scientific American* carried an article in which the author "proved" that the Ruby-Throated Hummingbird can't make that flight. Remarkably enough, it can and it does, disregarding that investigator's conclusion

But, oh, it's a pretty notion: A hummingbird nestled in the downy feathers of a goose or crane, probably in the non-smoking section, watching the movie and sipping a nectar-with-vodka, cruising down to Central America.

Bet the luggage goes to northern Mexico.

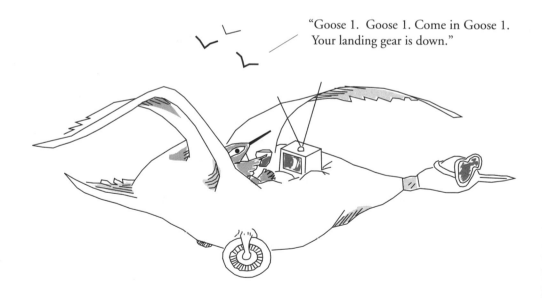

"Goose 1. Goose 1. Come in Goose 1.
Your landing gear is down."

Bum Rap

It struck me last week that most of the ospreys must have left for the year, and that magpies do good work. These deep perceptions came to me as I watched two magpies cleaning up an osprey nest. Can't think they would have been allowed in there if the rightful owners had been around. But couldn't help thinking about that housecleaning job. Leftover, ah, over-ripe fish parts. Leftover pamper-equivalents which failed to make it over the edge. A variety of creepy-crawlies.

A lot of people think they don't like magpies. Magpies get a bad rap, in part because they take eggs and small birds' young during breeding season. But mostly they eat insects. They also eat mice and snakes, carrion along and on roads, and carcasses of predator kills. The remains. Magpies even eat ticks, right off the backs of elk and deer and moose and bison and cattle. Got to feel good about something that consumes ticks.

Magpies get a bad rap, too, because large domesticated animals suffering from open sore or cuts have been pecked at and severely pestered. Deaths were reported and, in a few cases, substantiated in the first decades of this century. Supervision of valuable domestic animals has eliminated these rare instances.

Magpies are in the crow family. Smart birds. There are two species in western North America, the black-billed and yellow-billed. We have the black-billed magpie here; the yellow-billed is restricted in range entirely to California.

Magpies are large black and white birds with exceptionally long, wedge-shaped tails. A magpie's tail is longer than the rest of it. Seen up close in good light, the birds are iridescent greenish-black. In flight their white wing patches seem to appear and disappear, and their silhouette resembles a prehistoric flying dinosaur. Or perhaps an intercontinental bomber.

Blackbilled magpies are with us all year long. In winter as many as four dozen birds may flock together. Magpies kept as pets by humans will imitate human speech; wild flocks keep in communication with constant chatter.

Tip 'o the hat to our tuxedoed, feathered friends. They are good-looking, intelligent creatures who mainly do good work. And that one pair sure seemed to enjoy cleaning up that osprey nest.

Of course, they didn't have to do windows.

•

The Great Feather Caper

On September 18th, the Firehole River in Yellowstone National Park was covered with white feathers so thick the mass resembled foam. Feathers by the thousands upon thousands. Feathers — dare I say — by the millions.

Feathers floating downriver for 45 minutes without an end in sight, from Middle Geyser Basin north to the meadows where buffalo calves summer. Feathers 1 $\frac{1}{2}$ to 2 inches long; a few smaller, none larger than 3 $\frac{1}{2}$ inches. Remarkably uniform. White, some white with a tinge of gray at the tip. No flight or tail feathers. Down feathers.

Hmmm. Disease? Not likely.

A late fall molt? Unheard of.

Natural calamity? Well, there *was* this hot occurrence in '88 but...nah.

The great sleeping bag debacle of 88?

Lousy procurement specifications for the Wilson Chicken Fry?

The biggest pillow fight of the century?

Unfortunately, evidence of this remarkable phenomenon didn't survive—unless somebody finds feathers sticking to his waders. Or notices 500 naked birds.

•

Bad Breath

At the last Jackson Hole Bird Club meeting the featured talk was about dinosaurs. One sure thing about the club: the odds against any evening's discussion relating to birds is about 10 or 11 to one. (Why, then, is it called the Bird Club? Well, it started out that way, and once having achieved international fame and notoriety, it's hard to change. You know how it is.)

It was a darned good talk. Peter Moyer, an amateur paleontologist, was sailing along, commenting on the bird-like characteristics some dinosaurs exhibited, when he mentioned the hoatzin.

The hoatzin is the one bird species living today known to retain certain dinosaur-like features. Young hoatzins have functional claws at the ends of their wings and clamber about in bushes and shrubs. They nest over water, so this is a handy capability to have. Young hoatzins can swim underwater before they can fly, but this isn't a unique trait.

What is unique is that hoatzins are the only known birds whose diet is primarily green leaves. To subsist on it, they have a digestive system akin to that of a cow or deer: Hoatzins are ruminants. They have enlarged crops and esophagi where bacteria ferment the plant matter before it is passed on to the intestines. As a result of this digestive process, the birds' breath smells like fresh cow manure—an attribute that has earned them the nickname "stinkbird."

That aside, a hoatzin is pretty nifty. Rudimentary claws. A ruminant. A voice that is a cross between a peacock and an alligator. Size of a small turkey, but with a spiked hairdo. Hoatzins range from the Guianas to Brazil. What with the bad breath and all, it seems unlikely they will be imported to transplant in the valley.

A pity. Although the other day I did notice a certain apparition sporting a wild plumage, spiked haircut, and clutching what could have been a slice of tree trunk in a claw-like grasp. It was waiting in town for a bus.

Didn't check out the breath.

•

Obviously

A query from Brian Schwarz: When Geese fly in a V-formation, why is one side longer than the other? Answer: Because there are more geese on that side.

•

What's a bird to do?

A pair of Canada geese often nests along Flat Creek in North Park at the edge of Jackson. Their young are proudly paraded to admiring park visitors. This season the geese and smaller birds were inhibited from nesting in their customary locations because of construction work. Instead, the geese built a nest on the earthen roof of the Wyoming Highway Information Center adjacent to the park.

I'm told by a reliable source that the *News* was besieged by phone calls, faxes and e-mail from kind-hearted souls concerned about how the baby geese would reach the ground.

They jump.

Wildlife Management

Quack

The U.S. Fish and Wildlife Service recently released a memo which reads:

"Hungry predators, given the opportunity, frequently will eat duck eggs (and, if possible, the duck). Eggs eaten by predators have an unacceptably low likelihood of hatching. Ducklings not hatched are not known to fledge. Ducks that do not fledge make no contribution to the fall flight."

I like to think this is a spoof, somebody's attempt to make at least one current government revelation or pronouncement lighthearted. But the correspondent who provided the above—who has been a non-shadowy consultant in Washington for over 35 years—assures me it's bona fide.

•

Predator Control

The federal government has been in the business of killing livestock predators since 1915. The methods used have been of broad scale and non-selective. In 1989 alone, government hunters killed 86,502 coyotes;1,200 bobcats;7,158 foxes; 273 mountain lions; 236 black bear and 80 gray timber wolves.

We live in a technological age, and so the killing has become ever more efficient during three-quarters of a century. Poisons, helicopters, aircraft, and better weapons are now the tools of this sad trade. Control efforts have been limited almost entirely to ways and means of wholesale slaughter.

Now come a few wildlife specialists to teach farmers how to trap and kill the specific animals causing a problem. Now come Forest Service personnel in Idaho who show sheepherders how to use guard dogs and, by so doing, lose fewer lambs to predators. Now comes the State of Kansas, which teaches sheep ranchers to use pens to keep coyotes from attacking their flocks. Now come llamas to act as sheep protectors.

What will they think of next?

•

"We have no evidence..."

"No matter how cynical you become, it's never enough to keep up."
— *Lily Tomlin*

Fair warning: If you should read this column and accept its premise, you may alter forever your interpretation of how people in the hot seat present their positions.

Certain it is that when Meg and I came to realize the awful, deep meaning of their deception, we could never again listen to the never-ending, interminable so-called debates, hearings, public inputs, etc., to which an involved citizen can subject him or herself.

This revelation is as follows: When an agency, corporation, designated expert witness or an individual testifies in these familiar terms, "I (we) have no evidence of that...," you can be certain the utterer of that seemingly straightforward phrase never, no how, really and truly looked for that particular evidence. Or he looked the other way.

Tobacco companies that declare they have no evidence that cigarettes cause health problems didn't look for the evidence. Government entities which dutifully, if not willfully, fill in Environmental Impact Statements by saying, "We have no evidence that paving over brown peonies will affect the population of this rare plant..." may not be knowledgeable. Or truthful. Believe me; I have the evidence.

Highly paid, self-styled experts who testify they have no proof that a 10 to 20 percent rate of population growth has negative by-products such as crime increases, taxation rates...and on and on and on. Examples are almost without number — but my desire for further cataloging has suddenly vanished. Besides, I want to tell you what started this whole annoyance.

It was this item in the Wyoming Game and Fish Department News, dated July 7,1994:

CHEYENNE — Included in the comments the Environmental Protection Agency has received on its proposal to ban the manufacture of lead sinkers is a letter of concern from the Wyoming Game and Fish Department.

"As an agency that serves Wyoming's anglers, we felt compelled to let the EPA know that, at least in Wyoming, there is no biological basis for the proposed ban," wrote Joe White, G&F deputy director. "We (G&F) have no information, data or any other indication that lead sinkers have resulted in the death of any bird in Wyoming."

Because sinkers are an important component for anglers, White would like to see another metal, with similar properties and cost, developed before a lead ban is considered.

"We'd go long with the ban if a suitable replacement for lead is available," wrote White. "Until then, because there is no scientific information to support it, the ban would constitute an unwarranted burden on the fishermen and women of the state."

Classic. "We (Wyo. G&F) have *no information, data or any other indication* that lead sinkers have resulted in the death of *any* bird in Wyoming." (Emphasis added.)

Two comments:

▸ Lead is known, absolutely and with certainty, to be an environmental poison both in elementary form or in certain compounds, whether as sinker, shot or automobile batteries. Spreading it widely and casually where wild creatures must go to survive is obviously to be avoided.

▸ Deleted.

•

Stuffy

When considering the bison matter in Jackson Hole years ago, I suggested that the simplest thing to do was to rename the National Elk Refuge, "National Elk and Bison Refuge." Then the bison could legally hang out on the range. Problem solved.

My idea was largely ignored but not — to my amazement — entirely forgotten by the authorities.

Next, Meg and I proposed that a program be undertaken to reduce the size of bison in Jackson Hole. Horses, pig and some canines have been miniaturized. Why not bison? Not only would they be cute, they would be incapable of goring horses or competing with elk for food. They might even make good pets. That concept received only — well, how should we put it — contemptuous disregard. At best.

This week we proposed that bison hunts be carried out only by persons riding bareback, on horses they owned, wielding only spears.

Our correspondent considered the idea possibly unworkable. Oh, heck, he was more forceful then that—but this is a family newspaper.

Gee whiz. How stuffy can these bureaucrats get?

•

Proud

Biologists in Alaska have fitted 25 wolves with radio collars. Ordinarily, radios are put on various creatures as research devices. This time the idea is to afford aerial shotgunners a simply way to track and kill entire packs of wolves at a time.

Now that's a model, I suppose, of how to incorporate new technology into an activity while simultaneously ignoring widely disseminated knowledge gained by predecessors. Plus, I guess, the splendid idea that since the Lower 48 states screwed up on wolves, then it's all right for Alaska to do it, too.

Makes you proud you're not just a dumb, brute, lower animal.

•

Cry Wolf

Headline: Astronaut David Wolf Goes Aboard Space Mission MIR for Four Months.

Space cattle and sheep interests have protested to NASA and to Congress, fearing that this is just the first step toward the introduction of wolves to other planets.

And even beyond.

Extinction

A finality forever

The last passenger pigeon on earth died September 1, 1914. Eighty-three years ago. Her given name was Martha. She lived the final 15 years of her life in the Cincinnati Zoo, in captivity. Alone. The last of a bird species which once was the most abundant on this planet.

Until the 1850s passenger pigeons lived by the billions in the dense deciduous forests of America's east. Their habitat was largely destroyed: the birds shot, their nests robbed for human and hog food. With Martha's death they were extinct by 1914. And we weren't really trying.

Martha is now in the United States National Museum of Natural History. As a specimen, a reminder of how quickly a species can be lost. And how finally.

It might be a good idea for United States Senators and Representatives to go over and visit Martha. Particularly Western Republicans. Particularly those who want to undermine important protections in the Endangered Species Act. Or encourage development in public lands, including wilderness areas and national parks. Or refuse to provide funds for acquisition of California's Headwaters Redwood Grove, Everglades restoration and the Yellowstone mine. And in general ignore environmental promises.Just kind of look Martha in her glass eye...and catch your own reflection.

Gone

The last, the very last, dusky seaside sparrow died. A male, he died in captivity. Exactly when he died doesn't matter. Doesn't matter if it was a Wednesday in June, a season when he might otherwise have been carrying food to offspring. Or January. Or 2019.

It does matter that a species is gone.

Dusky sparrows were specialists in a world that increasingly favors the generalist or, perhaps more properly stated, the opportunist. Duskies liked and needed one strip of eastern coastal plain, and evolved to live there. Or nowhere.

Man's way of using that area, including the space program, changed it so the little dusky sparrow was doomed. Just a matter of time. There have been no female dusky sparrows known to exist for half a decade or more, and now the species is gone.

Biologists report that the rate of species extinction—animals, amphibians, plants, insects—has increased speadily to now reach one a day. One a day, and they don't make 'em like that no more.

We must applaud and support all efforts to preserve individual species. Man and his activities aren't responsible for the extirpation of every species lost, but man is thus far the only critter who can consciously eliminate another. And consciously try to save another.

It really is not a wild-eyed notion to help preserve an eagle or crane, an odd little flower, butterfly or reptile. It may even be a noble thing to do. And so damn tough. It's hard to get the biology correct: ask the locals involved with black-footed ferrets, grizzly bears, peregrine falcons, whooping cranes, bald eagles and trumpeter swans.

It's hard to get the commitment for long-term funds and sustained effort, even for the highly visible species mentioned above. Imagine if you wanted to save something with an unfortunate name, like lousewort.

It's emotionally exhausting.

And it's worth it all. Species preservation needs all the brains and money and heart that can be infused. Each victory, each entity not lost becomes even more precious, as so many others are lost everyday.

My field notes don't represent a systematic regional, let along continental, survey. Notwithstanding, for a discouraging long time they have reflecting a dwindling number of many birds, insects and mammals.

Life for a species isn't anymore than life for an individual. As those dang environmentalists keep trying to say, it can all happen to man. We pollute our water sources, are flippant about opening holes in the protective ozone layer, and poison the air we breathe.

Man, too, is mortal. Gone on a day in June. Maybe a Wednesday.

Volunteerism

Points of Light

Late in 1993 a calculated, politically motivated attack on volunteerism took place in the U.S. House of Representatives. This particular onslaught was aimed at volunteers in biological sciences, including ornithology. Against volunteers, amateur or professional, who participate in Christmas Bird Counts, in breeding bird counts, and in spring bird counts. An anti-volunteer provision was included in HR1845, a bill to establish the National Biological Survey.

The provision was sponsored by Rep. Jack Fields (R-Texas) and Billy Tauzin (D-La.), whose complaint is that volunteers, especially non-scientific volunteers, have a "special agenda" and that, in essence, "We'd be creating an environmental gestapo that will go on people's private property." If enacted, this will prevent the Biological Survey from using data provided by volunteers.

I'm really disturbed. I thought we were points of light, fur Pete's sake, doing wise things. Heck, I think of myself as emitting at least a kind of mellow glow now and again.

And I have this concern: One in five Americans volunteers a portion of his time — not to mention his money — to an enormous spectrum of causes. Birdwatchers are, of course, easy prey. People who can laugh at the sight of somebody else slipping on a banana peel get quite a tickle out of their fantasies of what birders are like. But — after all of those little old ladies in tennis shoes are put in their place and dispatched — who shall be next?

•

Subjective Bias

One of America's prides, volunteerism, is under fire again. All you hospital volunteers, or museum volunteers, or fireworks volunteers, or service group volunteers, beware. You are in danger of being accused of bringing "subjective bias" to your donated time.

You hospital volunteers, are you certain you simply want to help in the healing of the sick or hurt? Are you sure you don't have some hidden agenda?

How about you service clubs? Are you quite sure you simply want

135

to help burned kids or veterans or deliver Christmas toys to needy kids, and not to twist some fact around for an ulterior motive? And you museum docents: What secret motivation are *you* concealing?

Gee whiz. Start to believe in secret agendas harbored by volunteers, and one would then have to believe politicians might have rigid party lines they follow in a somewhat bovine fashion.

Say not so.

"Tell me, Mrs. Goodwill, what is the *real* reason you became a candy striper?"

Civility

Public Threats

Donald Oman is a forest ranger in the Sawtooth National Forest in neighboring Idaho. Not your average forest ranger, one concludes, for of Don Oman one of his detractors recently said, "Either Oman is gone (that is transferred) or he's going to have an accident. Myself and every other one of the permit holders would cut his throat if we could get him alone."

That's Winslow Whitely, a cattleman, talking thataway. When asked if he was in fact making a specific, public threat on Mr. Oman's life, Whitely replied, "Yes, it's intentional. If they don't move him off of this (Forest Service) district, we will."

That's not nice. What could a Forest Service officer possibly do to warrant a threat like that?

Well, it seems Oman is interested in not having the range under his jurisdiction destroyed by overgrazing, and in having the grazing contracts he must supervise complied with. Oman wants fences in repair and water holes fixed, as required by contract and regulation. He wants the number of cattle agreed upon to be the number of cows he can count.

It is, of course, in everyone's interest to keep the land in good shape: the cowman, the rangers, the public. It is, after all, public land.

It all sounds so discouragingly like the Chico Mendes affair. Mendes was a union leader turned enviro-realist in the Brazilian rain forests who sought to stop slash-and-burn forestry practices, to limit strip-mining, to stop the deliberate killing of indigenous Indians. Death threats were made against him. A couple of years ago, Mendes was gunned down.

Working together cooperatively, even when it's in everyone's best interest as it is in the Sawtooth's, isn't as popular as big time posturing and blustering. But it'd be nice.

Before anybody else gets hurt.

•

Renewal

When uncivil politicking makes you irritable and causes a chafe, which of course it must, hours spent outdoors will renew your spirit.

Dawns are nice. Dawns which put the lie to the old saying about red skies in the morning, sailors take warning. Dawns which don't.

Daytimes are pleasant. Elk coming onto the refuge. Antelope not ready yet to migrate, waltzing about still on the west side of the river. Quiet days. Clear, low streams. Although most deciduous trees and shrubs are hunkered down for the winter, a few stand out bravely here and there in fading glory.

Evenings are laudable. Sometimes highlighted by fierce sunsets, deepening from orange to plum, through indescribable bronzes, purples, mauves and peaches.

Nighttimes. Chilly, often clear. Planets and stars pop out. A waxing moon, full tonight; probably the harvest moon in some parts of the country, a hunter's moon hereabouts.

Oh, heck. Stay inside and trash your radios and TV.

•

Unacceptable force

Recent TV news broadcasts have shown videotape of police in California calmly applying pepper spray into the eyes of citizens protesting a logging operation. The victims scream and writhe in pain as the police — secure within their uniforms — methodically go about their business.

It is revealed that their actions are routine procedure in that part of the United States to curtail what is deemed by police not to be peaceful assembly. Peaceful assembly, you will recall, is one of the rights guaranteed all U.S. citizens by our Constitution.

Watching the spray being administered to protesters — who were politely sitting down — I was reminded of concentration camps, inquisitions, of torment throughout recorded human history.

This video should be played in schools, churches, public assemblies, libraries and police training academies as a forceful reminder: Torture of citizens by their police is unacceptable.

Celebrations

Bill of Rights

1991 was the 200th anniversary of the Bill of Rights. In 1987 one of those ubiquitous polls reported that 59 percent of Americans could not even identify the Bill of Rights.

What the heck, the Bill of Rights can't be all that important. Free speech. Free press. The right to keep and bear arms, specifically with regard to a well-regulated militia. Some stuff about protection against unreasonable searches and seizures. The right to a speedy trial. The right in certain instances to trial by jury. Various petty matters like those. Why, if things like that were all that important or significant, they would have been in the Constitution right off the bat.

Oh, yeah. The Constitution:

❑   I know what it is.
❑   I don't know what it is.
❑   Undecided.
❑   A new rap group.
❑   Don't care.

Check one box only.

•

Thanksgiving

The Puritans argued about whether Thanksgiving should be a feast or fast, even though they pretty much started it all with a feast. That first feast was in 1621; by 1685, the Massachusetts legislature couldn't agree on what to give thanks for. Some wanted a fast first, then a feast. Of course, some wanted the feast first, followed by fast.

This who's-on-first argument lasted almost 200 years. Then, on October 3, 1863, Abraham Lincoln proclaimed the last Thursday of November as a day of "Thanksgiving and Praise to our beneficent Father who dwelleth in the Heavens." Time to feast.

And so it was.

Thanksgiving was re-arranged in 1931 when Franklin D. Roosevelt moved the holiday to the third Thursday in November, on the notion that Americans would start their Christmas shopping early. Business interests were pleased. Sports fans, however, "threatened to vote Republican if

Thanksgiving Day football schedules were disrupted," according to Professor David Hackett Fisher of Brandeis University.

This would never do. And so, in 1941, Congress moved Thanksgiving back to the fourth Thursday in November, where it remains to this time. Although some folks are still confused.

Feast has won. Third or fourth Thursday is settled, at least for now. Time to talk about the important stuff: White or dark meat. What kind of stuffing. Cranberry sauce or jellied cranberries. Pumpkin or mince. Who gets to pick at the carcass.

You know, the real issues.

•

Wandering holidays

It was splendid of several of our past presidents to have their birthdays on Monday or Friday so that sometime in the future, patriotic Americans could enjoy three-day holidays. A couple of them even agreed to merge birth dates. A bit odd, but quite sporting, don't you think?

Recent presidents have issued declarations establishing Thanksgiving, Memorial Day, Labor Day, and July 4th at a more convenient time. Since even they won't mess with the birth date of the Big Guy's No. 1 Son, Christmas has stayed put.

But grown. Remarkably, Christmas sales pitches begin the day after Halloween. By the time Thanksgiving rolls around, most people think the holiday must surely be over. Alas, it isn't. The "X" number of shopping days left 'til Christmas has just made them catatonic.

The expansion, of course, is tied to a huge consumer spending orgy driven by retail stores—which hope to make up to half their yearly income during the holiday "season." Sort of like hunting season. The retail hunters "ho-ho-ho", and us sitting ducks "oh-no-no."

Getting a load of buckshot via non-stop advertising certainly opens my wallet.

New Year's Day has secured its place in the holiday line-up by virtue of position. It's hard to mess with the first day of the year. People will celebrate January 1, 2000, as the first day of the new millennium whether it is or isn't. (It isn't, really, but that's another story.) Americans stopped celebrating May Day when the Commies usurped it, using that innocent little holiday to display rocket launchers in their annual Moscow May Day parade. No more dancing about the May pole for Meg and me.

Be thankful National Pickle Week, Cowboy Mime Day, International Migratory Bird Day, and Take an Intern to the Executive Suite Month don't wander about the calendar.

Let's hear it for National Old Geezer Season, which precedes the Cardiac Arrest Festival. Held around the Vernal Equinox, every year. Like it or not.

Do come.

•

Veteran's Day

On Veteran's Day 1992, a ceremony was held to rename a particular national historical site in Montana the "Little Bighorn National Battlefield." The site is where Ogalala Sioux and Northern Cheyenne defeated George Custer and 267 soldiers of the U.S. Seventh Calvary in 1876, losing an estimated 100 warriors themselves.

As one might have anticipated, the renaming ceremony was controversial: It had to be postponed from its original July date because there had been believable threats of violence from both the people who approved the name change and those who opposed it.

It will be interesting to see how long it takes to refocus attention away from George Custer to the actual fighting at Little Bighorn River and its historical significance. I predict it will take at least as long as it has taken me to accept calling Armistice Day by its newfangled name.

All of this reminds me, I dunno why, of Marcus Reno—the Major Reno who missed Custer's last stand. Reno was in the class of 1855 at West Point. He didn't graduate until 1857, the result of having accumulated 1,031 demerits—an academy record that stands to this day. During the Civil War, Reno was leading a calvary charge when his horse fell and pinned him. For that he received a citation for gallantry, a recommendation for promotion, and a hernia.

I thought you might want to know.

Sports

Lou Gehrig, My Hero

My big brother taught me baseball. He was right about almost everything concerned with the strategy and play of the game. Of course, I had to perfect my understanding here and there for myself. You know how it is.

I honestly don't remember whether my superior baseball-playing sibling influenced me to admire Lou Gehrig as much as I do. It's likely I needed no direction. A boy chooses his own idols.

Lou Gehrig is, and will remain, an idol of mine. Sure, I know that Cal Ripken Jr. will, in about a month, eclipse Lou's record of playing 2,130 straight major league baseball games. Ripken is a heck of a player. He'll probably smash Gehrig's record and make it to 3,000 straight games. But he's not my "Iron Horse." I'm not a kid anymore, looking for a sports hero.

There was a lot more to Gehrig than his streak. He played with great players and, although overshadowed by the likes of Babe Ruth, he just went on doing his best, day after day. He could hit, but he had to learn to field and understand baseball strategy by constant practicing. He never quit practicing.

Gehrig benched himself after 2,130 games. His body quit on him. He couldn't hit. He couldn't play his position. He could barely shuffle. His problem was ALS, amyotrophic lateral sclerosis. Lou Gehrig's Disease, a form of chronic poliomyeltis that involves motor pathways of the central nervous system. On that day nobody knew what he suffered from. But he knew, everybody knew, he couldn't play ball again.

Lou Gehrig was 37 years old when he died.

Even if you're too young to remember when baseball was played in the light of day, on grass; when there were at times two full games played on a given day; when the long-ball wasn't the be-all of everything; when the pace of the game with its rituals, pauses, consultations, etc., added to the full enjoyment of what is, after all, a game—even if you have never watched a baseball game, you've probably seen black-and-white movie snippets of Gehrig's farewell address to a full Yankee stadium on July 4, 1939.

Surely, too, you've seen on film the famous 1932 World Series home-run promise by Babe Ruth when he, Ruth, indicated he would hit the next pitch for a home-run. He delivered.

Gehrig was the next batter. He congratulated Ruth, and the Babe said, "It's your turn kid."

Gehrig didn't point. But he did hit a homer.

·

Ripken

Cal Ripken went and broke the baseball-games-played-consecutively streak, going three for five with a home run on the day he tied Lou Gehrig's record, and two for four with yet another homer the next day. Then he gave a sensitive, thoughtful address to the crowd, to the nation.

Ripken probably should run for president. Mebbe with Colin Powell.

Of course, he'd probably have to give up his night job.

·

False Start

Occasionally in modern Olympic games that require a mass start, contestant eagerness, nervousness or anxiety results in false starts. One or more athletes anticipate the sound of the starting pistol or gong and launch into motion. All are called back for a restart.

In the Panhellenic Games of ancient Greece, as far back as 340 B.C., a different starting system was used that eliminated false starts or the possibility of someone deliberately getting a jump on his opponents. The contestants would crouch forward, restrained by two cords stretched tight across the starting line. One cord held them at their waists, another held them at their knees.

All the cords were held by the starter, who stood in a shallow pit some 25 feet behind the starting line. The cords passed through wooden posts at both ends of the line. After shouting *Apite!* (Take off!), the starter would release the cords and the wooden posts and cords would fall forward. Off the Olympians would go, covered with oil and unencumbered by clothes.

In modern experiments confirming this discovery, a reproduction was tested by runners. They didn't get tripped by dropped clothes; right-handed runners would miss each cord, whereas left-handed runners would step on each cord but not get tangled up.

Must be. Otherwise they would have been called the Olympic Tangles.

•

A Silver

Tommy Moe of Jackson Hole finished 12th in the men's Olympic downhill skiing competition at Nagano, the race in which he won a gold four years ago. He finished a tough course, one many skiers couldn't handle.

No medal is given for the end maneuver of downhill and similar ski races — you know, that dramatic flourish after finishing: slide to a halt in prime camera range, glance at the timer board, slip magically and with incredible rapidity out of at least one ski, and hold it up so the whole world can see the ski manufacturer's name or logo. No telling how many practice runs it takes to pull that one off well.

I award Tommy Moe a silver medal in that event, despite the fact that I've forgotten who made his skis.

Kind of orange, I think.

Mental Health

I'm okay; you're okay. But everyone else...

Let's see now. One of five Americans was abused as a child. One of five American children lives with one or more alcoholic parents, immediate family members, or guardians. One out of six is functionally illiterate. Six out of ten are overweight. (No one knows what percentage is too thin; they slip through the cracks.) Half of the people getting married will divorce. Almost everyone gets just enough misinformation from TV to reinforce his prejudices.

That leaves you and me.

I'm not so sure about you. Or me.

•

You can't get there from here

On National Depression Day (honest, now — it's October 6), I called the advertised toll-free number. 1-800-789-8900. I was curious to find out where the cheery National Depression Day folks would direct a depressed person in Jackson, Wyoming, for help. Just in case, you understand.

I was greeted cordially. I gave the operator my zip code and was promptly referred to three outfits. All in Idaho. Thinking that odd, I asked whether there weren't mental health professionals or organizations in Wyoming she could recommend.

Operator: "Wyoming, Colorado?"

Me: "Huh?"

Operator: "Wyoming, Colorado?"

Me: "No. No, no. The State of Wyoming."

Operator: "Wyoming, Colorado?"

Me: "No. Listen, lady, there are 50 states. One of them is W-Y-O-M-I-N-G."

Operator: "I'm sorry..."

Me: "Lady, where *are* you?"

Operator: "I'm in Colorado. And I've had a long day."
(It was 4 p.m.)

Me: "Well. Gee. Wyoming abuts Colorado. Sort of to your north, and —"

Operator: "Oh. Yeah. Cheyenne."

Me: "Well, do you have any suggestions for getting help in Wyoming?"

Operator: "No, sir."

At least she didn't say "Have a Nice Day."

•

A Small Quirk

It's almost predictable these days that following some violent act in which a citizen shoots up a train, fast-food emporium or post office, the media ferrets out the accused's neighbors and ask them to describe him. (Not often a her; just wait.)

The responses fall into two general categories:

▸ "Oh, he's just such a quiet fellow. Keeps to himself. Never noticed anything unusual about him." Or

▸ "Never did like him, but never spoke to him. Kept odd hours and dressed strangely. I think he read books. Never saw him wash his car."

Neighbors of Jeffrey Dahmer, the serial killer-cannibal, added a fillip, remarking that they had noticed on occasion (19 times) an unpleasant odor emanating from Dahmer's apartment.

Now there's the friend of a John Salvi accused of shooting and killing two young women in Boston, wounding five other people, and — a day later — shooting up a building housing a women's health clinic in Virginia. The good friend, John Cristo, is quoted by the Associated Press as saying: "There's nothing wrong with John whatsoever, other than he killed a couple people."

Well, I guess. Everybody has some little quirk or other.

•

Prison Guard Mentality

Put a uniform on a person or give him a title and it changes him instantly, subtly or overtly. I've seen an ordinary citizen metamorphose into a prototypical politician — primarily interested in office for narrow, short-run interest rather than governing or service — immediately following election or appointment. You have, too. I once watched a guy chosen by lot to be leader of a small group of movie extras change into a "prison guard" in a matter of minutes.

An example of this transfer of status via position and not ability has remained with me. It was a time I could still get in or out of a vehicle with a degree of nimbleness, but preferred to leave a bit of parking distance between my vehicle and an adjacent one. I viewed it as a matter of decorum, as well as a disinclination to scratch either my person or my vehicle.

Well. The Muse and I were going to a play and trying to park in a crowded lot. An attendant was in charge. When I say "in charge," I mean *in charge*. He directed me to move closer to a parked car. I did. He directed me to move closer. I backed up and repositioned. No good. He redirected me — with an imperiousness of unimagined majesty — to move even closer, standing were he wanted me (the customer, don't you know) to be. No matter what.

I put my left front wheel on his foot. I asked him, with exquisite politeness I'm sure, if that was sufficiently close. He nodded, noticeably less grand. I considered leaving him imprisoned there until we returned from the performance but alas, Meg made me back off.

I had a really good time at the play.

Personally Speaking

Growing Up

Lesson Learned

The only ethics lesson I ever needed I learned when I was about eight. Tall for my age, I was running with kids a couple of years older than I, and got challenged by them to shoplift in a Woolworth's Five and Ten. (Really, a nickel and dime store.)

I went in and tried to pocket something or other and all at once bells started ringing on cash registers throughout the store. Commerce stopped as every adult in the joint stared at me. A store clerk grabbed me, and didn't let go until a policeman arrived. The cop talked to the man for a minute then took me outside, holding my arm.

"I know who you are," he said. "Your father works around the corner, doesn't he?"

"Yessir."

"Now, just what would he say to you if I told him you were stealing?"

I realized, in one of those rare insights, that my pop would be angry and very disappointed in me. I'd been taught by example and lesson not to lie, cheat or steal. Shoplifting would not be condoned. (I spoke in this fashion even as a child.)

Besides, I'd be really punished.

So I pleaded, "Please, please, *please* don't tell my father. Please, please. I'll never steal again. Honest."

The nice, smart, clever cop let me go. And never told my father. Thus ended my shoplifting career and all the ethics lessons I ever needed.

Ethics is that simple. Do what's right in every situation. If you don't know right from wrong by the time you're about 12, you're in trouble. I remember looking at the inside cover of my first chemical engineering textbook and reading the "Code of Chemical Engineering." It took two whole pages of small type, and what it boiled down to was, "Do what's right."

So when I read about lawyers, engineers and the like beginning to *talk* about a code of ethics for themselves, I assume its too late for them. If a person doesn't know right from wrong and live that way from puberty, well, forget it. Signing some document isn't going to instill a visceral, reflexive knowledge of correctness. It must be learned by instruction and observation from a most tender age.

For me, an official hand on the shoulder accompanied by a significant frisson of anticipated parental disapproval settled forever any notion of questioning the correctness doctrine. The strength of that lesson surfaced years later when, in a weak moment, I decided to earn a professional engineering license. Since it had been some time since I'd taken a formal test, I fortified myself with coffee and had my slide rule at the ready. First, however, I was shown the Engineer's Code of Ethics to sign should I pass.

No sweat. I already lived that way.

Thanks, Pop.

•

Out of the Running

From what I remember of my childhood, I was a relatively sheltered kid. Wasn't allowed to swim: Polio scare. Couldn't have a bicycle:

Traffic. Incredibly, roller skates were permitted. Privileges were given when earned or not deemed hazardous. I'm sure I escaped the boundaries now and then, but not often.

And so there I was, ready to graduate from high school, never having traveled more than 150 miles from home, inexperienced in the ways of the world, but accepted as a contestant for 100, full-tuition, four year scholarships granted by Cooper Union. In those days a Cooper Union grad was almost certain to be sought after. And it was within commuting distance. A deal.

So, I turned up one summer morning at the examination hall to take the first of four days of tests. I joined a large group of, what looked to my 16-year-old eyes, adults milling about. There were no females hoping to become chemical engineers. There were just guys. Guys smoking cigars and pipes, wearing suits and ties, and carrying long, slim brown leather cases. Sometime later I learned the cases contained things called slide rules.

Nervous, I approached one of the guys sporting a mustache, slide rule, pipe and briefcase, and anxiously inquired if he was there to take the examination. My query was met with icy disdain. Seems he had gone to a two-year prep school just to study for the test.

This wasn't confidence-building information.

To make a four-day story short, I gave it my best shot but missed. Came in 110th in a field of 1,100 — unless all the losers got identical letters. Not bad, but no celebratory orange juice.

I wasn't downcast long. Longer than four days, but not long. Not at 16. It worked out for the best. I truly didn't want to live at home during my college years. And, Meg and I met at another school.

But I do remember.

Meeting Meg

It is a Broadway maxim that male and female leads "meet cute" in romantic plays. The circumstances of their first encounter must be unusual, memorable, or humorous. The psychologist and lady of pleasure each need to reupholster his and her sofa, and the furniture gets mixed up in delivery. You get the picture.

There was a play in which Jayne Mansfield—a voluptuous woman if there ever was one—poses in a bathing suit, dragging a towel as she complains, "Sand gets into *everything.*" I've never been certain if this scene adheres to the "meet cute" dictum, but it is memorable. Actually, it's all I recall about the play. Whatever its name was. Make of that what you will.

Anyway, when Meg and I met, the circumstances were definitely not cute. We were both freshmen at a small college in the East. I won't reveal just how long ago that was, but she and I were each tall enough to get notice. We may have been the tallest people then enrolled. Nowadays we're routinely towered over by seventh grade giants. With mustaches.

Meg was living in an off-campus, converted private home that housed 11 other female students. I resided in a rooming house two blocks away with roughly the same number of guys. I'd noticed Meg, of course. Even now I tend to notice tall women. I forget why.

Cutting to the chase, someone got the idea for an exchange dinner between the two places and, more or less by consensus among the planners, the tall people were slated to be dinner companions. I picked Meg up to walk her to my rooming house. We said hello or the like, and headed to my place of residence. On the way, we had to pass by a little shop bedecked with an awning. A low awning. Low enough that anyone tall would bonk his head. I'd gotten used to swinging out towards the street at that particular spot. This time, however, I didn't swing far enough, soon enough because, of course, Meg was at my side. (I'd been properly taught that males walk nearest the street to protect females from horses and vehicles. No one mentioned awnings.) The tall, previously silent, unhappy-looking girl at my side finally jabbed me with her elbow and snarled, "What are you doing? Trying to walk me into that thing?"

The evening's conservation went downhill from there. The other woman at our table tried to be engaging, but when her date literally ate peas lined up on his knife, and in general behaved badly, everyone lost interest in happy chit-chat. We just wanted it to end.

I wish I could remember how it was Meg and I started to talk that evening, but we did. We talked and talked and talked until the chaperone called time. Meg says the next time we saw each other I threw snowballs at her. If she says so, it must be so. I do recall telling her that when she came up the street with her dorm mates she looked like a hen with a brood.

Slick, hey? Almost as good as eating peas from a knife.

But we met again and again and well — to steal a line from a lesser-known personality — you know the rest of the story.

Hmmm. Maybe it was cute, after all. We're still talking.

Career Notes

Knee-patting

In the 60s I had, in my profession as a chemical engineer, the opportunity of giving technical and layman talks about pollution control. Mostly water pollution matters.

Often I'd start by pointing out that each and every person in the audience generated 150 to 200 gallons per day of polluted water. Sewage. If treated in a secondary sewage treatment plant, that generates approximately .2 gallons a day of sewage sludge.

And that, folks, is about a fifth.

People can visualize a fifth.

Today I'd probably have to convert to the metric system, and the small jocularity would lose its punch.

My punch is largely gone, also. I used to speak and write about how our environment was being increasingly polluted — not because of a lack of technology, but because of a management gap. I wasn't arguing against technologic advances; rather, I testified that our pollution abatement philosophy should be to clean up all wastes and effluents to the maximum extent possible, while new science was being developed and proved. Our standard should be fresh air, pleasant vistas and clear, clean water.

The above comes from testimony before Congress in 1966. A chap representing the pulp and paper industry who did not endorse my philosophy followed me. While we were sitting together waiting to speak we of course chatted.

After semi-listening to me for awhile he put his hand on my knee, leaned closer, and intoned — as did so many sanitary engineers of that day — the accepted doctrine: "Young man, it may be s—t to you, but it's bread and butter to me."

This witticism, and knee-patting, has gone on at every sanitary engineering function I ever attended, from conferences, plant demonstrations, to dinner affairs. A real yuk.

Thirty years later I could probably give identical talks about water pollution. I won't. There has been no real new technology in sewage treatment. Management hasn't improved. Moreover, I reached the maximum human tolerance for hands-upon-the-knee punditry a long time ago.

•

The Shunning

During my career I watched with increasing distress as leaders of an industry with which I was affiliated financed a deadly attack on Rachel Carson's book, *Silent Spring*, which detailed the effects of DDT. The publication prompted great disagreement between chemical producers and those who believed DDT's unexpected side effects were threatening various animal and bird species with extinction. Those, who like Meg and me, watched helplessly as robins convulsed and died.

In one editorial tirade on the matter, the *Chemical Engineering Journal* published a graph purporting to show a direct correlation, starting with the end of World War II, between tons of DDT applied and the number of cattle in the U.S.. No other factors, such as the end of the war — when attention to farming and other normal concerns could be freely given — were mentioned. A rather significant oversight.

This last straw for me resulted in my writing a letter to the journal's editor decrying its anti-Carson stand. I also provided a curve which "proved" a direct correlation between tons of DDT consumed and the number of VW (bugs) registered in the U.S., naturally, post-war.

The graph and letter were published. It did not do good things for my career. Perhaps the best I word to describe it is "shunning."

Oh, well. They stopped using DDT in the U.S., didn't they?

Pets

Best Friends

The Muse had a dog and a cat when she was growing up. I never had a pet, if you exclude a couple of goldfish and the occasional turtle. I certainly exclude them.

But when we were first married a cocker spaniel puppy wiggled her way into our lives. Blonde, irresistibly cute, a snap to train, lively, cheerful, smart and eager. She gave us enormous pleasure and love for over 18 years. We, in return, gave her love, security, food, exercise and constant attention to her every need, real or imagined. I'm convinced we got the better end of the deal.

Except for three months during which we were thoroughly miserable, wandering about asking strangers if we could please pet their doggies, we haven't since been without a cocker puppy. Puppy No. 5 presently owns us. Also blonde, cute, sprightly and eager. Standard cocker traits, yet an individual in her own right.

We take our puppies everywhere we can, and to a few places where they were or are barely tolerated. We have rationalized our travel plans to include only those places to which we can drive. Our first dog flew once. On the return flight we looked out our plane window to see puppy No. 1 in her crate on the tarmac as the DC-3 was starting to taxi. Fortunately this was long before security checks and FAA guards at airports, and yet more fortunately, Meg's sister spotted the puppy and immediately grasped the situation. I can still visualize Nancy running out in front of the moving plane, stopping it, and refusing to let it proceed until the pup was on board.

So, we never did that again. Puppy No. 1 enjoyed riding on the parcel shelf of our first car, a '36 Chevy coupe with a rumble seat. Once, when Meg and I were driving along engaged in a discussion about certain laws of physics, I attempted a demonstration and hit the brakes. The puppy flew out the window onto the roadway, somehow unhurt. She never got near an open car window again.

Dogs, unfortunately, have shorter life spans than humans do. And so, love lavished regardless, they die before we do. It's agonizing for us; dogs accept it with dignity given half a chance. More dignity, more serenity than we muster, I'm damn sure.

The ache doesn't ever quite go away, but a new cocker puppy makes it much, much better.

Bless them all.

•

The Idiot

The winter of 1964 we kept in our home a crippled little wild bird —

or anyway part of one. He was tailless, had one useless wing, and for a while he cared little for the business of living. He was a *Dumetella carolinensis*, a catbird.

The catbird is one of the more familiar North American songbirds, found in cities and suburbs and on the farm, inhabiting dense shrubbery, splashing in birdbaths, darting across streets and lane. Its note is a nasal, petulant cat-like "meeway." Its song, however, is full and rich, sweet and varied, altogether musical.

The catbird is smaller and slimmer, by just a little, than a robin, slate-gray in color, trim and well-groomed. Both sexes are similar in appearance, each having a black cap and sporting a chestnut-red patch under its tail. Only the bird watcher is likely to notice that under-tail mark, or to know that other well-known representatives of the family *Mimidae* include the brown thraser and storied mockingbird, or to care especially to mount an expedition to capture this or any other three-ounce bird.

But I do, you see, because I'm a bird watcher.

Catbirds migrate south fairly early each fall, typically by late September in the northern states. But what came to be our catbird had been reported skulking in a thicket a month or so after the rest of his kind had left Cleveland, Ohio, for the winter. Bird watchers hear about such things, and then go look for themselves. And so I did.

For a reason I couldn't define, I found his physical appearance as well as his belated presence odd. I slowly approached him as he sat on a bottom branch of highbrush cranberry.

He didn't fly away.

I stepped closer still, and when he didn't move, put out my hand and slowly, slowly reached for him until I touched his small tail.

He moved convulsively and his tail came off in my fingertips. I was astonished. The catbird was rather upset about the whole matter, too. It dawned on me that the oddity of his previous appearance was that his tail assembly was askew and about to fall off. It explained his remaining late into the fall; he couldn't fly. His tail was gone and I could see now that one wing, his left, was almost featherless and limited in movement. He was a prisoner, restricted by infirmity to a single thicket.

I tried to grab him, but whatever had possessed him originally to let me touch him no longer operated, and he fled by hopping from branch to branch to the inner sanctity of his refuge.

Later that day I discussed the situation with several bird watcher friends, and got them to agree to help me rescue the bird the following morning. Meg and I have harbored a series of injured birds, and felt we could care for one more. At 7:30 the next morning, then, we gathered, four adults of mature physical age and a 13-year-old boy.

The bird was still in the hawthorne-cranberry thicket, a copse about 30 by 50 feet. He was ready for us. For 20 minutes we hurled ourselves into the underbrush, grasping and clawing at a mite of a bird that couldn't fly but could certainly hop and jump and dart and scurry. The chase finally ended only because of the boy, who squirmed under the lower tangle and trapped the catbird under his cap.

Exhausted, the bird and we rested for a time. Some minutes later we put the thoroughly frantic creature into a small cardboard box lined with shredded newspaper and took a look at our prize.

He was ruffled and unkempt, panting from exertion and fright. His cap was dirty. Cowering in a corner of the box, without his tail, he looked almost like a mouse. Just half a bird.

We took him home, not at all sure we had helped this little guy after all. He huddled on a perch in his brand-new circular cage and drooped, listless. He refused to eat and generally moped. Operation pamper went into effect. Meg tempted him with sliced apple and blueberries. I found the one pet shop in town selling mealworms and tweezed those into the cage. We vitaminized his drinking water and made him a tepid bath. We fed hardboiled egg, mashed in pablum, with milk. We tried various positions for his cage, letting him see other birds at the outdoor feeders if he

wished. He was safe and warm and had food. But he seemed resigned and apathetic, and we feared he was in that not un- common wait wild birds sometimes enter before succumbing to quiet death.

It was a month before he began to perk up. Mysteriously, he be- gan to preen and bath with gusto, getting him- self thoroughly sopping, head-to-tail wet then me- thodically fluttering himself dry. He became active and responsive and began to eat better, growing from half to three-quarter size. As his personality surfaced we gave him an unglamorous but affectionate name: Idiot.

Winter deepened and Christmas approached. One dull afternoon we decided to cheer our home with carols and turned on the phonograph. During the third song a hesitant, tentative but harmonious song gently intruded upon the familiar one.

"Honey, the Idiot is singing," whispered my wife, grinning broadly.

It was as though he had caught the spirit and joy of the season. The Idiot sang and sang and sang. He sang in harmony with Christmas songs all that afternoon, falling silent only when the records changed. He changed his tempo with each song, singing in definite rhythm and filling the room with his exuberance. He relished carols but dug swing and related to opera. He sang to Benny Goodman and to Brahms. We later discovered he would even respond to singing commercials.

Thankfully, he was apathetic towards rock and roll.

Henceforth, the Idiot sang every morning, calling loudly at first light. He became active during the day and he sang to evening TV. He would rustle about his cage at odd hours through the night. During full moon, the Idiot didn't sleep at all but hopped through the dark until dawn. He ate and looked better.

We were unabashedly pleased at having saved him from freezing, and to have him regain the spirit to live. Selfishly pleased, perhaps, but we didn't care. He was our pet, our catbird, and we had brought him to health. There was song in our home.

We enjoyed hearing the Idiot sing, watching him bathe with abandon, feeding him tidbits. He was alert and interested in everything — people, other birds, movement in the yard or on the patio. We'd occasionally set him free on the screen porch to exercise, though we quickly learned not to do that immediately after feeding blueberries.

Our friends enjoyed him, too, bird watchers being especially enchanted. When he felt like it, he'd eat from our fingers. Once or twice he adopted a fixed posture, becoming an elongated extension of a terrified eye as a predator hawk passed through the backwoods. Birds can look fat or thin, ruffled or sleek, more or less at will. But this attitude of sheer frozen panic was unique and remarkably striking. He even began to scold our cocker spaniel, not his wisest move. Only elevation of the Idiot's cage achieved a tolerable truce.

The only real problem with having a caged bird came when we went out of town. Some kind soul had to be inveigled to bird sit. The Idiot had to be transported and fetched along with all of his paraphernalia: suet, frozen blueberries, apples, mealworms, vitamin drops, the cage and its stand, written instructions.

If no one volunteered for the job, we took him with us. The Idiot loved to ride in a car, day or night, and would crane his neck to peer about. Looking around, balanced on the highest perch he could reach, trim and sleek, he was a happy traveler. Our dog, on the other hand, hated the arrangement. She would have to be restrained, and would then spend the entire trip trying to extrude through her collar to attack the cage.

One summer morning Meg and I were enjoying a second breakfast on the back porch. The dog was toying with a couple of biscuits. We had our coffee, and were feeding the catbird blueberry halves from our fingers. It was a quiet, relaxed time and everyone was content. The Idiot hopped to his favorite perch, wiped his beak several times and sang a few soft notes. Then fell heavily to the cage floor, dead.

A young lad we knew who was studying to be an ornithologist performed an autopsy on the catbird. The Idiot had suffered a massive stroke, and died instantly. We were saddened at the loss of the Idiot. We wondered, as all pet owners do when death comes to their charges, if we had helped the little creature by caring for him.

Of course we had. He had no premonition of death and hadn't suffered. He had lived an additional nine or 10 months, not bad for a bird whose life expectancy might be only a couple of years in the wild, at best. His months had been carefree and without danger or want. He rewarded our attentions with song. We both benefited by our association.

Thirty years have passed, but we haven't met another Idiot we've liked more.

Pet Peeves

Customer Service

Pretty much, I've accepted that my role now is to be a consumer. And I do my best. I eat more than average and consume a bit of taxable sin-products. Admittedly, I don't hold up my end when it comes to electronics, say, or computers. Or clothes.

So I was rather proud when I found I needed a felt inner thing-ee for my boots. I called one of our premier shops in town. After the obligatory, incredulous giggle about my boot size, I was told:

- ▶ There are none in the shop anywhere near that size and
- ▶ No, we couldn't possibly order you one, you silly goose. We only order in quantity for tourists with average-sized feet.

I was miffed until I recalled that, of course, I didn't matter, being both a local and outside the normal size range. My task is only to pay for the infrastructure to accommodate those very tourists, and make store owners and developers even more wealthy. After all, Jackson is a place where you can get anything you want, but nothing you need.

The next call hit a place that required me to have a push button on my trusty, black, rotary-dial phone. This phone is an heirloom for heaven's sake, given to us by Don Ameche his own self. The message cut off, leaving me unable to communicate over my information dirt path.

Thankfully, I found my felt liners. Before spring.

The Waiter Code of Conduct

A phenomenon more unrelenting than gravity is the dependable vanishing of a waitperson who has been told you're not quite ready to order, never to be unearthed again.

Or beamed down, whichever direction waiters go to sulk and hide.

I'm confident you've undergone this experience. It makes little difference if you're in a humble cafe in Nevada or the spiffiest bistro in, say, Hollywood.

The code of the waiter is the same:

- The customer is here to accommodate my desires and schedule;
- The customer must close any conversation to respond to my interruptions without hesitation or hint of annoyance, if he *ever* wants to be served;
- The customer must be prepared, only seconds after having his plate plopped before him, to answer my inquiry, "Is everything all right?" and
- "Can I get you anything else?" must be uttered before the customer has had time to look at his plate.

A corollary to the Wait on Me Code developed during an energy crisis in the US of A. To save energy, water and dishwasher soap, a customer had to request a glass of water, a practice which yet remains. In keeping with the code, any customer requesting water now is treated as an outcast. Especially should he want his water in a clean glass.

Nothing can be about done this. Customers are generally too embarrassed to speak out. Besides, they're afraid the wait staff or kitchen help will spit on the salad. The restaurant owners are "managers," not "service providers." And the waiters are just putting in time until Hollywood finds them, Ed McMahon calls, a future love comes through the door, or the next shift arrives.

The only answer is to have a drink and order something that will take a little while to arrive…at least long enough for the drink to take effect. Dine alone or with someone whose conversation is interruptible.

Better yet, stay home and order a pizza.

•

The Grand Slam

There was a time when automobile advertising was dominated by the slamming of the car's doors. You could tell everything you needed to know about a car's worth by the solidness of the slam.

Door slamming, surprisingly, took hold of the American people. It has become so ingrained it will last forever — or until automobiles are made obsolete by a continent-wide traffic jam.

What? You don't believe Americans are in the clutches of a door-slamming fetish? Go to a campsite anywhere in the country in the morning, when people are awakening and striking camp, or in the evening, when people are arriving and setting up. The sound of doors being hurled into their jambs is as constant and ongoing as a chorus of agitated crickets. For some unknown reason, it has become impossible for a real American to open a door or hatch once, leave it open until one has removed everything needed, then close it. Impossible. The true, patriotic American must, simply *must*, open and slam each door in an ascending crescendo. It seems to satisfy a primordial desire to push something around, and announce to any person still sleeping at 6:10 a.m. that "I am here."

Trust me. I know.

One Size Fits All

One size fits damn near nobody. Face it.

More than the slogans "low fat" or "lite" or "reduced calories" deceive—far, far more—is the calculated infamy of "one size fits all."

Start with hospital gowns, where everyone starts. If I walk a hospital corridor in a gown, I need two: one facing north, the other south. I'd rather not sit in a chair of any mobility without a blankie. The dang things barely cover my thighs, let alone. Other guests of the establishment are bundled up in theirs like babes in swaddling clothes, dragging their tails.

Anybody here remember when Chrysler Corporation made automobiles that were "smaller on the outside, bigger on the inside."

Yah, you betcha.

"Is there a breeze in here?"

169

Without actual proof — which would require effort on my part — I believe manufacturers create items purported to fit all sizes based on the erroneous belief that everyone will then purchase their merchandise. This, despite evidence that millions of prospective customers on both ends of Raynes' Physique Bell Curve are eliminated from being contributors to their bottom line.

Remarkable. How could business folk have failed to notice that when clothing and shoes go on sale to clear shelves for new stock, what's left is predominantly average sizes?

And why is this so? Because, fer crissake, small people, short people, big people and tall people — and various combinations thereof — have snatched up everything miraculously, accidentally, made in their sizes.

•

Late

As Abe Lincoln remarked to a group of us one time, possibly as a rebuke, "I have noticed that the people who are late are often more jolly than the people who have to wait for them."

As usual, Abe was right on.

We live where "Locals Time" is regularly offered to excuse:

▸ Being late
▸ Unexplained absences
▸ Accepting a "better" offer with no apology to the expectant hostess and/or
▸ Bringing one, two or a half-dozen strangers along to the festivities.

Probably just like your hometown — unless you reside in some uptight, strung-out, high-fallutin' community where a sense of decorum and correctness may still linger. Some mythical town where meetings start on time, politeness and consideration are a way of civilized life, and children are all above average.

Being occasionally late is understandable. I've been late to things. Once — and I'm still abashed about it — I missed an affair in my honor by a precise 24 hours. However, being chronically or deliberately late, unreliable, or a predictable no-show is another matter. It says something about you.

And it may say something about those who patiently wait. If this is you, I say assert yourself! Your time is worth as much as the latecomers. Probably more. Start your meeting, your meal, your trip, your — well, you really can't start your doctor's appointment by yourself. Pity.

Go ahead; be prompt. Be reliable. Be prepared. Never forget a birthday or someone's anniversary. Show up at designated hours and places. If a no-show of repute is more than 15 minutes tardy, shove off.

See where it gets you.

I know where it gets you. The next time you're late or forgetful — as you will be — you're going to hear about it for a long time.

•

I Don't Know

Say anything except "I don't know." That's the credo of nearly every person who stands behind counters, answers business telephones, discusses menus, or provides information to an anxious or hopeful public.

That's the credo, indelibly fixed upon employees the moment of their hiring. Astonishingly enough, no training is required. Put the uniform on and bingo, they simply must say "I don't know."

Yet off-duty every waiter, store clerk and breathing guy or gal who has been in town for 24 hours is transformed into an authority on history, restaurants, motels, recreation, wildlife, places to see, places to miss, the best movie ever made, and what the weather will be for the next 18 months.

Kind of miraculous. Almost unbelievable.

Or should be.

The "I don't know" credo is most easily observed in civil service information venues. It is practiced by those who may in fact know the answer to an inquiry or could find it, but simply don't want to be bothered. This phenomenon reaches its pinnacle in national and state parks. Ask about a geologic artifact, and be told the geology ranger is off that day. Ask about a flower and be informed, with a shrug, that the flower guy is not in.

Want to have some fun? Counter that you are going to be here for a month and can come back. Sweetly ask when the flower guy will be on duty.

You win if a glint, a sparkle, a fractal of comprehension appears, however transitorily, in the eye of your servant.

Don't count on it.

Poison Ivy

Meg and I used to have a fishing camp just outside Adirondack State Park in upstate New York. It was a nifty little place with no electricity, a well we dug ourselves, and a companionable two-seater outhouse with red toilet seats. The one-room cabin was 16x16 feet, I think, and screened throughout. It was not, at first, bat-tight; bats zooming around in the flicker of kerosene lanterns grow large enough to fill nighttime imaginations.

There were no developments around our isolated setting. Our camp was perched on the bank of Schoharie Creek, a river in spring run-off that becomes a series of lacy, cobbled pools by early summer. Small-mouth bass and northern pike are sustained in its clear water.

We were wet-fly fishermen then, back when wet-fly fishermen were the acknowledged fishing elite and dry-fly guys were not an economic powerhouse. Meg tied flies to patterns that worked on our stretch of creek. We got so we knew which pools to cast to and how long a cast was required. We knew when the deer came to drink and where the osprey hunted, and to watch for the occasional bear.

It wasn't all idyllic. Nothing ever is. It turned out my observational powers weren't sharp enough to recognize leafless poison ivy. On one fine spring clean-up, fix-up day I stood downwind of a twig and branch fire and exposed my whole body to oily fumes of Rhus toxicodendron.

This was a mistake.

Itchy welts broke out all over my body. All. Over. My. Body. Clothing could not be tolerated. I took on the appearance of a large calamine lotion statue, and still could not resist the urge to scratch. I don't think the soles of my feet were blistered, or the inside of my nose and mouth. Those were the exceptions.

I've been quite susceptible to poison ivy attacks ever since. Once, some years, later, on a section of the Adirondack Trail in Pennsylvania where ivy limbs and roots the diameter of fence posts invade miles of stone walls, I got the itch even though I never came within yards of the stuff. Guaranteed.

Step ahead a decade. I caught the itch again, this time from an aluminum salt deodorant spray. I was declared a "dermatological emergency," of all weird things, and hospitalized. Released, I spent several days in the nude in a screened-in back porch in our place in Ohio.

It was a learning experience, for myself, and perhaps, the neighbors. I don't use deodorant to this day.

Sorry about that, friends.

A Special Easter

Sometimes a mis-adventure turns into a not-to-have-been-missed, unforgettable experience. One such event happened to Meg and me at the Grand Canyon.

We had diligently asked around before striking out over a 60-mile dirt road clearly marked on the maps with the warning: "Impassable when wet. Make local inquiry." No one we met except local law enforcement had ever been down that road. Ever.

Moreover, no one seemed aware of past or present weather, let alone a forecast. One shopkeeper did give us the frequency of a Las Vegas radio station he usually received after sunset. All we heard was a repetitive thumping noise known as rock 'n roll music — which I believe is responsible for almost all of the social ills of our society, including crime, incivility, poor schools, poor politics and, quite possibly, potholes. In any case, no forecast.

The morning sky was clear so we set off for the north rim of the canyon at Toroweap, our truck camper equipped with water, food, tonic, gin, books, field guides, and a cocker puppy. The basic necessities of life. We tootled along, enjoying everything in sight, not seeing anyone else until we reached the park boundary and a primitive campground. After leveling off we had lunch and investigated the canyon's edge. Far below was the Colorado River. Vulcan's Throne, an ancient lava plug, rose imperiously above middle of the river. Layers of time. Colors. Flowers. Birds. We soaked up Nature's silence, into which she contrived to put wind, bird song, and river sounds and still provide the solace of quiet. Magical.

It stormed early in the morning of our third day, a frightening cacophony of rain, lightning and wind. At first light a park ranger appeared urging the other party and us to get out while the getting was still good, or we could be marooned for days. He was persuasive; we packed up.

We drove perhaps 15 miles before getting inextricably stuck in muddy gumbo. On a flat section of the road. The goo instantly adhered to our boots, creating platform soles 8-10 inches thick. We somehow managed to get our rig to the side of the road and relaxed. Collapsed, actually. The rain did not abate until sometime that night.

Next morning was Easter. The road looked a bit better but didn't approach being navigable by our camper. Mid-morning, we first heard an engine, then saw an Army surplus 6x6 all-wheel-drive troop carrier swaying side to side on the muddy track. It pulled up and stopped. A smiling young man asked how we were, obviously relieved we appeared OK. He pressed six gallons of water on us, telling us where to leave the empties on our way north. Assured we were fine, he skidded off towards the rim.

A few hours later, he returned, this time with an invitation to Easter Sunday dinner and a celebration. Seems the "grandchildren" of John Riffey, a famed Grand Canyon ranger who had recently died, were scheduled to meet at the ranger station near the north rim to celebrate his years of faithful service, and drink a toast to his memory.

Riffey had befriended many river rats, and they considered him a favored relative. Among other things, he flew a Super Cub named "Pogo" from his own Toroweap International Airport, a familiar sight to North rim desert dwellers. Those celebrants who had made it in before the rain had food to spare and we were welcome to join the crowd at the ranger station; please come.

We went. The only thing we had to contribute was a bottle of gin and a few odds and ends, but there was ample provender and drink.

After eating and socializing we were, to our great pleasure, made "honorary grandchildren," and invited to visit John's grave. We stood in a circle around the modest site and passed a bottle. We never knew him, never knew his gathered relatives, who ranged in age from 20-somethings to grizzled geezers. But we truly felt part of them all. It felt proper, correct, to be there. Before leaving, the sun came out and a brisk wind picked up.

Just before dark we were taxied back to our rig and told that by morning the road would be passable. It was. We passed several delayed celebrants going south and a rescue party on horses searching for three people who had left their truck to escape on foot and hadn't yet surfaced. The road had a hazard or two but we made it just dandy. We left a heartfelt thank-you note with the water jugs.

We haven't been back to Toroweap. Perhaps we'll never return.

But on Easter Sundays we become John Riffey's grandkids again, and lift a glass.

Column Writing

Shoot the Editor

Almost every week I find my underlinings, my italics, my spacings, my capitalizations — my style, for Pete's Sake — reduced to straightforward type font. This means I have to try to describe my thoughts with clarity and precision. To write better. Is this something I should need to confront after so many years of columnizing? A little attention to all the advertised "bells and whistles" in the software would jazz the space up — but no.

Sorry folks.

•

Shoot the Editor: Part II

Last week, this column appeared on the front page of the Style Section of the *Jackson Hole News*. A signal honor, I am reliably informed. (Where are we appearing today?)

Not only that, but my photo was right up there, atop the prose, snapped out in the field doing something natural, a candid shot.

Right.

Actually I was holding my puppy, Hilary, and it was a portrait attempt. Hilary didn't make the cut; she got cropped. That's really too bad, in my opinion. The editors, a rag-tag band if ever there was one — albeit very merry — chose the wrong subject. I admit that Hilary's palimpsests are even more difficult to read than mine are. But she's been accepted into computer school, so there is, for her, hope.

And, of course, biscuits.

•

Kudos: Part I

It certainly is nice to find that one writes for America's top weekly newspaper (*The Jackson Hole News*, July 23 issue, front page). Shoot, I didn't know that. I'm partial to the *Oconomowoc Enterprise*, myself. I suppose with all the celebrating and partying, the big-award accepting guys haven't had time to thank all the little people without whom, why, it never coulda happened. Well for my part, I want to congratulate the big ones and thank my family, my faithful observers, all the birds and bees and furry things, my devoted readers, all the little persons at the *News*, and my one-member fan club.

•

Kudos: Part II

It's a pleasure to add my humble congratulations to all the accolades currently directed toward the *Jackson Hole News* and its many star performers. The *News* was named Wyoming's best large weekly for the second consecutive year, and awarded a slew of photography, advertising and writing honors. Those of us who toil anonymously to shore up the foundations from which the big shots spring buoyantly onward and upward are proud simply to be allowed to be a small cog for big wheels. It, um, is sufficient.

I'm proud to report that this column, too, has achieved a big honor. From the Composting Association of Federated Composters. The reward is for recycling. Specifically, "The Most Devilishly Clever Re-Use of Already Reported Matters of Interest in a Weekly Column Appearing in a Prize-winning Newspaper."

Don't scoff; there's a lot of competition.

•

Topic, Topic, I need a Topic

I have no real topic for this week's column. It's due on New Year's Day, for heaven's sake.

Here's something: Willem J. Luyten died in November 1994, at age 95. He was an astronomer internationally known for his work on stellar motion, the origin of the solar system, and dying white dwarfs — exotic stellar species of enormous density that give off little light. They are considered the final stage evolution of most stars.

Dr. Luyten once asked the National Science Foundation for funds to organize an international conference on white dwarfs. The request prompted a fiery letter from the then Surgeon General, who wrote, "Human subjects can't be used for experimentation, and federal money cannot be used for race discrimination."

Scary, huh.

•

A-ha! A Topic

To my amazement there seems to be an organization calling itself the National Society of Newspaper Columnists. Fancy that.

Putting aside my disappointment in never once having been solicited to join the National Society of Newspaper Columnists, I observed in an AP story that, at its recent and doubtless national meeting, the NSNC awarded a Mr. Kato Kaelin its "Sitting Duck Award." Mr. Kaelin used his allotted 15 minutes of fame in connection with the trial of Orenthal James Simpson for double homicide. He received the honor for being the best subject for a newspaper columnist who is without a clue as to what to write.

To quote from the award, Kaelin is "the target most useful to a columnist on a slow day." Well. Quack, quack.

•

A Mistake?!

I have in hand an Illeg-i-fax pointing out that I made a mistake several weeks ago when I wrote that a supernova that exploded in the Ursa Major constellation did so 12 million miles from Earth. An unnamed critic allowed that I had "just destroyed Earth," since the Sun is 93 million miles from Earth. The supernova was, of course, 12 million light years from earth.

Whew. I'm really doubly glad about all of this. First and foremost, I'm glad I didn't actually destroy Earth. There are so many others out there who, even as we speak, are doing a much better job of it than I ever could. Second, it has been so long since this column contained a mistake that much concern had been expressed in many quarters that it is infallible. Truthfully, it's a great relief to have my incredible string of perfect columns finally snapped.

Really, though: When you think of the huge staff involved in the preparation of even one of these columns, it is statistically improbable for there never to be some small misstep. There's the research group; the clip-

180

ping services; the gnomes who abstract thousands of periodicals, journals and technological articles; me; The Muse; typists, editors and self-styled journalists at various levels of Best Weekly Newspaper on Scott Lane in Jackson, Wyoming. Pretty tough to network all these without an occasional slip.

And yet, it has been so weirdly long since a misstatement that I guess one of those many heroic personnel cited above got just a little cocky. I trust my entire staff of co-workers and specialists is both properly chastened and properly thanked for the previous many long years of devoted service.

I thank also my unknown eagle-eyed reader and, as always, my dear friend Russell Baker.

·

Feedback

Writing a column is instructive — with luck for the reader and, for sure, the culprit concerned. "Far Afield" started out as a column about birds 20 years ago and gradually, well, wandered. More natural history topics were added, as well as a splash of politics and personal comments. It is, afterall, an opinion venue.

It's a matter of some satisfaction for me that it has an audience whose interests, loyalty and relatively non-critical acceptance continue to this day.

I did say relatively non-critical. At a book signing recently, a fellow came up, introduced himself as living in a city 500 miles distant, and declared that my columns put him to sleep. He went on to explain that his life is stressful. He reads my columns in bed because they relax him.

I think he meant it as a compliment. Come to think of it, it was a compliment.

Feedback isn't always easy to interpret. I've yet to classify a remark made to me by a passer-by of the therapy pool as complimentary or medical opinion. As I was being forced to "jog" through water by my Physical Terrorist, the woman approached and sputtered, "Why Bert, you look better than I expected you to."

I have had one unpleasant phone call about a particular column. The guy was apparently quite drunk and possessed limited vocabulary. I marked him down as non-appreciative.

I'm proud that some of my faithful readers are people whom I admire for themselves and their accomplishments. I try to write with their sensibilities in mind. It's pleasant when one of my close friends comments on topic or interest or style. I particularly relish it when some delightful nymphet says to me that she likes my work. Unfortunately, at this point in my life I can never remember her name. Occasionally, gentlemen also approach with some comment. I don't remember their names, either, but for some reason I don't find this as irritating.

Well, to be fair about it, can you expect a non-politician to recall the names of thousands upon thousands of adoring fans? Not hardly.

Self-Promotion

Buy, buy, buy

The word from inside the Beltway is that American consumers must get out there and spend, spend, spend. And do it right now, if you please. Another word from the same place is that Americans must save, save, save so there will be money to invest in businesses which, in turn, will create jobs, jobs, jobs.

The *sotto voce* in DeeCee is that rich Americans simply won't invest in America and thus build jobs, jobs, jobs so that employed persons can spend, spend, spend unless — and perhaps, until — they get increased capital tax benefits. Otherwise they will simply continue to invest in foreign countries. They may be rich, but patriotic? (Well, of course, patriotic. But not as a first priority.)

Well, let's not concern ourselves with them. Let us middle and low incomes spend, spend, spend. The buying season is here. Let's go down to our favorite bookstores and other civilized outlets and get us some copies of that beloved classic, *Birds of Grand Teton National Park and Surrounding Areas*, by moi. Rated the best buy in a survey of birdwatchers from all over the globe who have visited since 1984, when the book was made available to an anxiously waiting audience.

This act of great good sense, generosity and — dare I say? — patriotism on your part may not in itself get our beloved land out of its recession, but it'll be a start.

•

Shop, shop, shop

The designated Busiest Shopping Day of the Year has become, apparently, accepted nationally. Although presidents have yet to be coerced into issuing an official proclamation, I expect that practice will commence anytime.

In sympathy with such a glorious sentiment of the holiday season, I'm encouraged to indulge in a ritual of my own, and alert any of you who have thus far not purchased your very own copy of *Birds of Grand Teton National Park and Surrounding Areas* to get busy and buy one. It's a really fine book and makes the perfect stocking stuffer (for oddly shaped stockings). There are, in actual fact and by actual poll, 1,001 constructive, educational, recreational and mechanical things one can to with *Birds of...* Send $3 for a complete listing.

I have seriously contemplated that *Birds of GT, the Sequel* should be thicker than the first volume. I can't tell you how many readers have complained that it takes as many as three of *Birds One* to level the average restaurant table. Clearly an injustice.

In the meantime, while you and I wait impatiently for *Son of Birds* (a title I choose not to make into an acronym), go out and get yourself and each of your friends one of the originals.

Aging

✎

What's Goin' On

Once upon the New Year's, it was my custom to predict the comings and goings of natural history events-to-be for the forthcoming year — Uncle Bert's Almanac. Gave forecasting up a couple of years ago; U.B. can't even tell you what happened last week.

•

Misguided Park Policy

Somehow, in some devious and churlish bureaucratic manner, the parks (and forests, too) have stretched out once-modest trails to exhausting lengths; steepened the ascents and waxed the descents; and, not content knowing that the ozone layer is all messed up in the stratosphere, have reduced the oxygen levels in the air, causing one to have to breath heavily and pause frequently.

I hadn't fully realized the extent to which this misguided park policy has been taken until last week. My nature sorties are usually solitary ones — or with one or two carefully selected companions — near home. (Otherwise, I've discovered of late, I'm always scurrying vainly to catch up with the field on the field trip. Noticing mere wisps of girl-childs or male striplings sauntering casually off into the distance nonstop lost its fascination the first time it occurred.)

Last week I conducted a bird class in Grand Teton National Park for Teton Science School. The unfortunate ones who sign on expect a teacher to be up in the lead at least sometimes. The students were energetic young ladies ; it quickly became apparent I couldn't keep pace. Their idea of constructing a sedan chair to get me about wasn't a good one; they would have had a hard time bearing the thing and using their binoculars at the same time.

Maybe if they used a kind of shoulder harness, though...

•

Perspective

Having acquired a certain maturity I find that, surprisingly often, younger members of the populace aren't much interested in my ideas. Contributing to this, I suppose, is my habit of trying to lighten the atmosphere of meetings, conferences, retreats that use up perfectly good weekends, and dreary planning sessions, by putting as much whimsy and good humor into my thoughtful observations as possible. This sometimes leads my companions to question my seriousness.

And, too, I'm often impatient at many gatherings. They seem to go nowhere because no one runs them and those there have no real desire to accomplish anything. My impatience is not always successfully hidden.

What with one thing and another, I no longer participate in many meetings unless I'm a member of the audience. I get very few invitations to consult, advise, or serve as a director for a non-profit outfit. (Although I might consider a profit-making one...)

What's the problem? I have become semi-aware that younger people involved in matters of mutual concern consider me an Old Fogy. Me! Me, with all my learning, all my experience, all of my well-known perspicacity, waiting to be used, yet ignored.

All of which has me sadly wondering if I was a snotty, self-important know-it-all, don't-bother-me-Old-Boy punk once. Back when I was a flaming, out-spoken conservationist who wrote scathing editorials, gave inspirational talks, and worked to promote wise use of natural resources. Was I then insolent, pushy, ignorant of history, disrespectful?

Sadly, I believe I must have been.

Rewriting history is not an option for those of us without spin-doctors. If I sinned, I can't change what I said and did and wrote all that long ago. What I can do is try hard not to be one of those "gray eminences" of whom Robert Sapolsky has written, whose who become reactionary, "simply because they have the most to lose in the face of novelty."

And to issue a belated, sincere apology to those in whose footsteps it was a privilege to tread. Plus one to any whose feet I may step upon today.

So sayeth the Old Fogy.

The Check-Up

There are many imponderables in life. Close to the top of my list is how anyone bright enough to earn a medical degree can be so, well, dumb, when it comes to talking to his or her patient. Listen up white coats: The following phrases don't make our day.

▸ "Uh-oh."

▸ "That looks expensive."

▸ "Are you *sure* you feel all right?"

▸ "Perhaps you should put your affairs in order."

And then, of course, is my personal non-favorite. "People of your

"I'm afraid I have disarming news."

age should expect…" or its many variations. ("Did you think you could do that kind of thing forever?") Anyone lucky enough to reach that mysterious age—a sliding scale of 30 upwards, depending on the particular physical deterioration—doesn't need the effects of age to be articulated by their doc, or by a lab technician so young he frets about acne instead of wrinkles.

When you're having your eyes peered into, your heart and lungs listened to, your X's being rayed, and your mind being analyzed—all the while dreading hearing some awful diagnosis—it does not ease your psyche for the medical litany to begin, with a sigh, "Let's face it, you're officially a geezer, so it's not surprising…"

Not surprising that you need bifocals. Need expensive dental repair. Have less energy. Can't eat spicy foods. Are getting a belly. Have extensive wear-and-tear on this or that. Have reduced sexual desire. Can't cope. But, heck, did you expect to get out of all this without paying your dues?

Some "health providers" (Ha! False advertising!) have learned not to utter the like. Silence is certainly better than, "Look at so-and-so, he's hospitalized." Or, "You're not quite ready for the home. Hee-hee."

Trust me, these aren't thigh-slappers. We gray-haired, no-haired folks have that market cornered by personal experience. Heck, I'm considering writing a book titled, "Screw the Golden Years." Either that or "I'm a Full-Groan Man."

Not to be believed is the saying "You are only as old as you feel." You couldn't live to be that old. Nor the saying that a person can grow old gracefully. While aspired to, sometimes one just can't. And please don't refer to some extraordinary old geezer still able to compete in running, skiing or tennis, making us feel guilty if we don't rise out of our chairs and JUST DO IT. Give us a break, white coats.

Hands of Time

For reasons too depressing to recount, I make frequent visits to a physical terrorist clinic. The idea, I gather, is for me to maintain the commendable Reubenesque physical stature I've achieved, as opposed to any improvement. My motto: If you've got it, let it sag.

Physical terrorist clinics of my acquaintance have certain similarities, all designed to intimidate. One enters and is faced by machines lying in wait. Big machines. Chromed machines with welcoming names: Body Mashers. Steps to Nowhere. Total Wham. Fiberwrecker Metabolic Systems. Upper Body Extruder. Don't Dare Tread on Me.

The terrorists themselves are wonderful. Cheerful, caring, encouraging, very knowledgeable, untiring. They can't be blamed if body equipment designers come from SS troop lineage. Unless, of course, they design their own, one of which I call Black Ice.

As I say, I hang out in a P.T. clinic a few times each week. Others come and get better and eventually leave, but I go on like the Everyready™ bunny. Idly watching a fellow sufferer the other day, I made a serendipitous discovery, viz.:

Meg's and my interest in pictographs and petroglyphs is longstanding. Handprints are but one example of rock art that has been duplicated worldwide. Carved handprints, pecked handprints, outlined handprints, left-hand and right-hand prints, painted handprints. The prints, dating back 30,000 plus years, are found in caves and rock walls everywhere on earth. And on the walls of modern-day physical therapy clinics. Persons plagued with shoulder problems stand and push themselves away from the wall at about shoulder height, a procedure cleverly called "wall push ups."

This clearly is the reason handprint rock art appears everywhere.

Before steel, chrome and rubber came along, prehistoric physical terrorists had to make do with materials at hand. As it were. Rock faces, cave walls, boulders, stones, tree limbs. Nothing was sacred. Record of injured Cro-Magnons exercising their triceps, seriates anterior, and pectorals (not to mention the perineum) was writ in stone. Recognizable over the centuries. Tributes to care-providers of an earlier time.

An archeological breakthrough, don't you think? A mystery solved at long last. Now then, about those stick figures and wavy lines...

•

Boomers

"Baby boomers" — an appellation even worse than the degrading "Senior citizens" — have peaked and are on the steep slope down. At least that's what the advertising community has declared. The boomers are middle-aged. Tough truffles.

The ad folks believe the little fizzlers are catching on to the notion that perception is not reality, that it sometimes isn't even perception. That their gorgeous bodies will yield to gravity no matter what they do. That they are starting to comprehend that luxuries are just that, luxuries, and not their personalities, not their identities. That there might — just might — be more to life than things acquired. Well, I never.

•

Screw the Golden Years

Dear Reader,

By this time you will have decided that the easy flow of these essays indicates the author's complete grasp of subject, style, grace and enormous erudition.

Well, it's not so blame easy. In fact, it's terrifically hard work. Sometimes it never comes together. For example, for this book I wanted to write about reaching that "certain age." (At one time I wanted to write a whole book titled *Screw the Golden Years*, but the Muse sidelined the idea.) I collected artifacts of wit and wisdom concerning "getting on," but am bedeviled on how to incorporate them in an essay's short form.

Yet you should have the advantage at, um, your young age of these witticisms and truisms. So here they are:

▸ "One day you're a peacock. The next day you're a feather duster."
— Anonymous

▸ "To me, old age is always fifteen years older than I am."
— Bernard Baruch

▸ "The aged gentlemen waited for the strolling youth to stroll on to the next thing, for the wisdom of age had taught them there was no folly greater than seeking to enlighten the young before age had placed humility in their hearts and gray hairs in their mustaches. This was the wisdom of James Thurber, who had said, 'Youth must be served, frequently stuffed with chestnuts.'"
— Russell Baker

▸ "Old age is a shipwreck." — Charles de Gaulle

▸ "If you only want to prove you're alive, a touch of pain will do the trick. But if you want to live, love." — Roger Rosenblatt

▸ "The trouble with being old is there's no future in it."
— Edna Frederikson

▸ "And they lived happily ever after, except for the age thing."
> — A *New Yorker* cartoon

▸ The three stages of life: Youth. Age. "You look great."

▸ "One of two advantages of getting old is that you can—if you are unable to stop it—evaluate people and situations with increasingly good success. I forget the other one."
> — Bert Raynes

▸ "If you are going to get old, get as old as you can."
> — Ansel Adams

▸ "Everybody has got to die, but I have always believed an exception would be made in my case. Now what?"
> — Official last words of William Saroyon

▸ " The dream, though old, is never old...Did you see an old woman going down the path? I did not. But I saw a young girl and she has the walk of a queen."
> — William Butler Yeats

▸ "See, the problem with doing things to prolong your life is that all the extra years come at the end, when you're old."
> — *New Yorker* cartoon by Mankoff

▸ "Our machines have now been running for 70 or 80 years and we must expect that, worn as they are, here a pivot, there a wheel, now a pinion, next a spring, will be giving away."
> — Thomas Jefferson to John Adams

▸ "I promise to keep living as though I expected to live forever. Nobody grows old by merely living a number of years. People grow old by deserting their ideals. Years may wrinkle the skin, but to give up interest wrinkles the soul."

—Douglas MacArthur

Well, you can easily see that the opportunity to use these and many, many other observations on aging, grouchiness, hope and despair would have made *Screw the Golden Years* an immediate success. Another classic.

Alas. We shall not know.

•

Hummin'

Busy as a bee. Busy as a beaver. Work, work, work from dawn to breakfast. No doubt you can still keep up with your job or hobby or lifestyle and attend meetings, serve on committees, get to all the many social functions and civic affairs each day presents, do spring cleaning, keep up with your correspondence and demonstrate impeccable family values.

In a former life, so did I. At my peak I could do four things at a time and be in a couple of places at once. Now, I either forget about the opening and traditional whatzis, or I neglect to recall that the not-be-be-missed dothingy was scheduled yesterday. On occasions, I write down an invitation or date; I more and more often lose the loose note. I yearn for the next step—simple enjoyment of my irresponsibility. At present I feel vaguely guilty.

But I have discovered a palliative for my unease. I sit down beside a pile of unread must-read books and journals and watch ice cubes melt in a soothing beverage. Cheers.

Musings

There's a new vehicle being offered by a Japanese automaker. It's a small delivery van called the S-Cargo. (If the Japanese start getting funny, too, American car assemblers are in deeper doo-doo than we thought.) The S-Cargo strongly resembles a motorized snail; has large, mournful, bulging headlamps; stands six feet tall; and sports rainbow-shaped windows and a sunroof.

Sounds like the real me.

•

Readers will be happy to know a certain Barry Fox — who describes himself as an author, a chancy occupation these days — studied bottled mineral waters and found no reason to believe the notion that, "The real secret of Perrier's taste is that the water leaches through a mass graveyard for victims of the Black Death." Barry is probably right. Besides, that was the 14th century. Be happy. Don't worry.

•

Sam Donaldson, a reporter on TV: "The ugly catfish has become the food of choice of the beautiful people."

Meg: "They'll eat anything."

The bed sheet industry failed to notice—for over a dozen years—that mattress thickness doubled in that time span. Sleeping themselves in hammocks, one presumes, bed sheet manufacturers continued to crank out sheets the same size they always had. Nancy Butler, vice president of communications for the International Sleep Products Association, recently admitted, "There's no question there was a real communications gap between the sheet makers and the mattress industry." Perhaps somebody was asleep at the switch.

●

Throughout the let's-do-it-in-the-off-year congressional machinations about salaries and ethics, I kept wondering if it can possibly be ethical to take a salary—let alone a salary increase—to become ethical.

●

Did you read about the two left behind World War II Japanese soldiers who decided not to return to Japan after 45 years of fighting with Communist insurgents in Malaysia? A matter of honor. The sister of one, long awaiting her brother's return, remarked, "I did not hear from him in nearly 50 years, so of course I was worried."

A guy gets busy with this and that.

●

An item in the Santa Clara, California, *Press Democrat* reported that licking toads—cane toads, to be precise—is the latest way to hallucinate. In San Francisco, of course. Cane toads apparently secrete a hallucinogen called bufotenine, a legally controlled substance. Cane toads, however, aren't controlled. They can be bought in California. Now then, is that irresistible or what?

This cries for investigative reporting, surely. Who was — or is — the first guy to lick a toad to experience what would happen? How many species did he experiment with? How did he get anyone else to, ah, imitate his technique?

Actually, this calls for a documentary.

•

President Bush designated the 10 years commencing January 1, 1990, as the decade of the brain.

Inside the Beltway, too?

•

A slogan from The Muse as we motored through the forests of the Northwest. Muttered she: Keep Japan green. Clear-cut America.

•

Apropos of nothing very much are the results of a toxicity test conducted almost 90 years ago by the then Bureau of Chemistry, a branch of the U.S. Department of Agriculture. Under test was "Butter Yellow," a coal-tar product then being used as a food color. The test subjects were dogs.

My pal, K.M. Reese, relayed the results:

"One of the dogs was given three grams of Butter Yellow on May 6, 1903. This produced a few hours of vomiting and other adverse symptoms —

such as loss of appetite — but the animal gradually returned to normal during May 9-15. On May 16, the dog got another three grams of Butter Yellow. The notebook entry for May 18 said, 'Vomiting continues[1].'"

Footnote[1]: "This dog ran away."

•

My brother lives in the mysterious East; sweet guy, he thinks I live in the mythical West. He recently sent me a photograph of a sign which appeared in his ocean shore community, pleading with me to give an explanation. It reads: Parking for Drive-Thru Patrons Only.

Well, no, Frank; I can't. But I'll ask around.

•

Ad in the Thrifty Nickel: "Almost brand new (worn only three times) beautiful wedding dress/veil. Must sell." Probably put on a little weight.

•

In a journal I would probably stop reading except I get it gratis as an *Emeritus Member* — which title certainly sounds a lot grander than it is — there was an ad for a brand of bathroom tissue said to be "Made from 100 percent Post-Consumer Waste."

Hmmm.

"Say, honey, what do you suppose..."

The Muse: "I hate to even *think* what that might mean."

Right-o.

Headline in last week's paper spoke of "moose jams." Tenor of the story suggests that stopping to view wildlife in a national park is really a bum idea.

Well, how about that. Here I am, in my simple way, thinking that stopping to look at, and take pictures of, a moose or scenic vista is one of the very things people ought to do in national parks.

Doggone. I'm *always* on the backside of every great social issue.

•

It certainly looks as if the military portion of the Iraq/Kuwait/Persian Gulf Affair is a wrap. The hardest part lies ahead. We've been cautioned not to "feel too much euphoria." Apparently, euphoria is in the air, rampant in the land.

Funny thing, I never caught it; I kind of wish I could at least have had a 24-hour bout of it.

I try *so* hard to be up-to-date. Guess I shall have to be content with my daily self-prescribed dose of liquid euphoriant. During which hour I shall toast my old pal, Freddy Nietzche, who often remarked over a libation or two, "Whoever fights monsters should see to it that in the process he does not become a monster."

He might have had something.

•

Following the riveting first hours of statements and allegations of sexual harassment by Professor Anita Hill, a TV network aired a Revlon nail polish commercial urging women to "Yo! Come on Move it...Shake your Body, Shake your Boddee…" The exhortation was coupled with sub-liminal images of evocative posturing by lithe, young females.

Insightful programming.

•

Weather persons must believe skiers are so unthinkably dumb they must be reminded constantly, each and every time there's one snowflake, that snow is the preferred medium upon which to do their little thing.

Boring.

•

Those interchangeable male TV anchors on CNN seem abruptly to be changing their hair from gray to brown or black. Overnight. The Muse says it must be a new policy or Dye or Die.

•

It's National Potato Lovers Month again. The Muse, surprised, exclaimed, "Already? Why, it seems like just yesterday…"

•

The media—blessings be on them—inform us that serial killer Jeffrey Dahmer always wore a condom when engaging in sex with his victims. It certainly is reassuring to learn that the message about safe sex is getting through.

Thanks to C-Span 1, I've recently had the opportunity to hear and see former aspirants for the presidency deliver I-give-up speeches. Their statements were good-humored, self-deprecating, smart, witty, thoughtful, insightful, considered, patriotic, even charismatic. They were darn near inspiring.

Makes you wonder why they simply don't campaign that way.

•

It has now been found that if you cook in a microwave, you only need to wait 30 seconds after eating to go swimming.

•

I'm pretty upset that nobody—not one of my four favorite bookstores—asked me to review a new publication entitled grandly, *Sex*, by someone who calls herself "Madonna." So, instead, I've become rather a follower of other reviews.

They have not been raves. The best one-liner I've come across was penned by Vicki Goldberg, who writes for *The New York Times:* "I don't much care what Madonna does so long as she does not do it in the streets and frighten the horses." Of course, Vicki was paraphrasing Mrs. Patrick Campbell, who in fact said, "I don't mind where people make love so long as they don't do it in the streets and frighten the horses." Mrs. Campbell was a British actress for whom George Bernard Shaw wrote the role of Eliza in "Pygmalion." Thereafter the two were close for decades. Despite his renowned curmudgeonly behavior.

Writing in *The New Yorker*, Calvin Tomkins noted that *Sex* not only breaks no new ground, "it tumbles kerplop into the pit of glumness that swallows ninety-nine percent of the world's would-be pornographers. It is boring, non-erotic, and dumb." Tomkins concludes his review (in what the magazine calls its Department of Advance Warning) thusly: "Sadly, her book is going to give pornograhy a bad name."

Sex comes wrapped in plastic. Usually that's done to protect the contents from being despoiled. In this case it may be to protect the potential reader.

•

A good friend gave me a report of a recently organized winery tour in Napa Valley, California:

Tour Guide: "Just to get an idea of how knowledgeable this group is about wines, I was wondering if anyone here knows two different types of wines."

Tourist from Wyoming: "Red and white."

Tour Guide: "That's a very common answer, but not correct. Anyone else?"

Second Wyoming Tourist: "Corked and twist-off tops."

Tour Guide: "Please return to the bus."

•

It is an established political law that if you have only a left wing or right wing you're going to fly in circles. But with two strong wings you can fly straight into a wall.

My brother, who is something of an iconoclast, envisions a new bumper sticker: "Your Night to Call Telephone Solicitors."

·

Does anyone recall a cartoon about the philosophical quandary of whether a tree falling in the forest—where no human is around to hear—makes a sound? The cartoon settled the matter for me: It does. As it yields reluctantly to gravity, the tree mutters, "Oh, Darnnnnn."

·

What I assume is an unofficial, non-US West phone directory appears each year in local mailboxes. Useful and handy unless your mailing address is incorrect, in which case it's a long-term pain. This year's cover features what appears to be a pregnant bull elk. Inside, a yellow page ad for Flat Creek Motel, opposite the National Elk Refuge, proudly states there's a view of "Elk Refuse" from every room.

Well, I guess.

·

As I write, it is being debated whether there will be a partial "shutdown" of the federal government. I'm glad I don't have to agonize over whether I'm essential or not. A poll was taken among my friends and family, and I've been told where I stand.

I heard it was close.

Did you watch any of the NASA conference during which they discussed evidence that a primitive life form once existed on Mars? Data collected by vastly improved technological devices was disclosed and discussed.

Notwithstanding, the slide projector operation proceeded as slide projectors have ever since they were invented: out of sync and imperfect.

If they can't run a slide projector can we believe the Mars stuff?

Probably. Slide projection is — by evidence gathered for decades — more difficult.

•

To Whom It May Concern:

Will anyone who has slept in the White House bedroom please tell us if the bed is extra long? We assume it is, but you know: for that kind of money, a person likes to be forewarned.

•

A relevant remark, sure to become a collector's item, from Robert Wilensky: "We've all heard that a million monkeys banging a million typewriters will eventually reproduce the entire works of Shakespeare. Now, thanks to the Internet, we know this is not true."

•

In an article by George Steiner which appeared in the *New Yorker*, was this quote from the monastery library of San Pedro in Barcelona, Spain. It refers to the stealing of books:

"For him that steals, or borrows and returns not, a book from its owner, let in change into a serpent in his hand and rend him. Let him be struck with palsy, and all his members blasted. Let him languish in pain crying aloud for mercy, and let there be no surcease to his agony till he sings in dissolution. Let bookworms gnaw at his entrails in token of the Worm that dieth not. And when at last he goes to his final punishment, let the flames of Hell consume him forever.

Kind of makes a "Please Return to_____," or your basic "EX-LIBRIS _____," look pretty ineffectual, doesn't it.

•

Have you ever wondered why both serial murderers and college presidents are almost universally referred to by their first, middle and last names?

•

A train passing through Poland at night was running out of coal, and the engineer couldn't tell quite where he was because the lights in the area had been knocked out by a storm. He said to his trainman, " I think we're coming to Gdansk or Danzig (the German name). Let's send the porter out to buy more fuel. Can you see a sign on the depot that says Gdansk?"

"It's hard to tell," replied the trainman, "but it looks like Danzig in the dark."

Cried the engineer, "Buy coal, porter!"

Says the Muse:

Boom is not success. It's excess.

•

Considering that human beings are social creatures, we sure don't get along.

•

I love the environment. I live in it. I've always lived in it.

•

We've gone directly from the brave new world to the brazen new world.

•

On overwhelmed, overrun Utah recreation areas: " They're going to have to reconcile their recreation with their procreation."

•

Commenting on a new book, *Life: A Natural History of the First Four Billion Years of Life on Earth*: "You had to be there."

•

AP news item: One of five Americans don't know or aren't sure Jews were killed in the Holocaust, or that it happened in World War II. Said she, "One of five Americans don't seem to know about anything."

•

News item: Unwed Teen-agers kill baby after its birth in a motel. Said she: "Well, they can always adopt."

•

Says Bert: If a psychotic puts poison in a pain capsule, society is outraged and strong action is taken immediately. But if corporations, governments and rape-and-ruin types pour poison in our air and water, there are delays, variances, permits, extensions, and low-interest loans.

About the Author

Bert Raynes

Bert Raynes is a chemical engineer turned conservationist. Then turned amateur naturalist and author in retirement. No one knows exactly when he turned curmudgeonly; opinions vary widely. He sometimes still futilely resists the very idea.

Bert writes a weekly column for the *Jackson Hole News*. In addition to this book he has penned *Valley So Sweet, Birds of Grand Teton National Park and the Surrounding Area* and, with Darwin Wile, *Finding the Birds of Jackson Hole*. He lives in Jackson, Wyoming, with his beloved wife, Meg, and their cocker spaniel, Chelsea.

Order Form

To order additional copies of this book, please check your local bookseller. If not available, send a check or money order to: White Willow Publishing, 1255 N. Iron Rock Road #6, Jackson, Wyoming 83001, in the amount of $12.95 per copy plus $1.50 for shipping. Sorry, orders can only be filled in the continental United States. Please complete the information below:

Name _____

Shipping Address _____

City/State/Zip _____

•

Valley So Sweet, a natural history journal of Jackson Hole by the same author, is also available from White Willow. Please send $12 plus $1.50 for shipping/handling for each copy of the book to the same address.

White Willow Publishing
1255 N. Iron Rock #6
Jackson, Wyoming 83001
307-734-7002